Canadian Policy on Nuclear Co-operation with India:
Confronting New Dilemmas

Edited by
Karthika Sasikumar and Wade L. Huntley

Simons Centre for Disarmament
and Non-Proliferation Research

Vancouver, BC, Canada

Canadian Policy on Nuclear Co-operation with India: Confronting New Dilemmas

Edited by Karthika Sasikumar and Wade L. Huntley

ISBN: 978-1-4303-0811-9

Simons Centre for Disarmament and Non-Proliferation Research
Liu Institute for Global Issues, University of British Columbia
6476 NW Marine Drive
Vancouver, BC V6T 1Z2 Canada
Tel: 604-822-0552
Fax: 604-822-6966
Email: simons.centre@ubc.ca
Website: www.ligi.ubc.ca

Cover design by Industry Images, Vancouver

Acknowledgments

This publication presents the revised contributions to the namesake conference convened by the Simons Centre for Non-Proliferation and Disarmament Research in Ottawa on 19-20 March 2007.

The conference and publication were made possible by the financial and logistical support of the Asia Pacific Foundation of Canada, the International Security Research and Outreach Programme (ISROP) of the Canadian Department of Foreign Affairs and International Trade (DFAIT), and the Liu Institute for Global Issues at the University of British Columbia. Venues and conference hosting assistance were generously provided by the Canadian Centre for Treaty Compliance at Carleton University (19 March) and by DFAIT at the Pearson Building (20 March) in Ottawa.

The conference discussions benefited greatly from the participation, in addition to the invited presenters, of selected senior academics with experience in the area, and of representatives from the Canadian Department of National Defence and the Privy Council.

CONTENTS

Abbreviations

ABM	Anti-Ballistic Missile
ASEAN	Association of South East Asian Nations
AECL	Atomic Energy Canada Limited
AEA	Atomic Energy Act
CANDU	Canadian Deuterium Uranium (Reactor)
CCS	Cabinet Committee on Security (India)
CD	Conference on Disarmament
CIR	Canada-India Reactor
CIRUS	Canada India Reactor US
CTBT	Comprehensive Test Ban Treaty
DAE	Department of Atomic Energy (India)
DEA	Department of External Affairs (Canada)
DFAIT	Department of Foreign Affairs and International Trade
DNWS	*De facto* Nuclear Weapon State
EU	European Union
FMCT	Fissile Materials Control Treaty
GDP	Gross Domestic Product
GW	Gigawatt
GWe	Gigawatt electrical
G-8	Group of 8 countries
HMt/y	Metric tonnes of heavy metal per year
IAEA	International Atomic Energy Agency
IMF	International Monetary Fund
IR	Inferred Resources
KT	Kiloton
k$	kilodollar
MT	Megaton
MtC	Million tonnes of carbon equivalent
MTCR	Missile Technology Control Regime
MW	Megawatts
MWd/t	Megawatt day per tonne
MWth	Megawatt thermal
NACD	Non-proliferation, Arms Control and Disarmament
NAM	Non-Aligned Movement
NATO	North Atlantic Treaty Organization

NNWS	Non-nuclear Weapons State
NPT	Nuclear Non-proliferation Treaty
NRX	National Research Experimental Reactor
NSA	Negative Security Assurances
NSG	Nuclear Suppliers Group
NWS	Nuclear Weapons State
NWFZ	Nuclear Weapon Free Zone
OAS	Organization of American States
PNE	Peaceful Nuclear Explosion
PRC	People's Republic of China
PSI	Proliferation Security Initiative
PTBT	Partial Test Ban Treaty
Pu	Plutonium
P-5	Permanent (five) members of the UNSC
RAPP	Rajasthan Atomic Power Plant
RAR	Reasonably Assured Resources
RevCon	Review Conference
SNW	States with Nuclear Weapons
SSEA	Secretary of State for External Affairs (Canada)
SWU	Separative Work Unit
tU	tonnes of Uranium
U	Uranium
UK	United Kingdom
UN	United Nations
UNSC	United Nations Security Council
US	United States
USSEA	Under-secretary of State for External Affairs (Canada)
WANO	World Association of Nuclear Operators
WMD	Weapons of Mass Destruction

Nuclear Co-operation with India: An Overview

Wade L. Huntley and Karthika Sasikumar

On July 18, 2005, US President George Bush and Indian Prime Minister Manmohan Singh announced a bold agreement to restore US nuclear co-operation with India. In 2006 the two countries reached accord on more detailed terms of each country's expectations, and the US Congress passed enabling legislation that created an exception for India to the longstanding prohibition on US nuclear trade with states outside the NPT. At this writing, India and the US have just concluded grueling negotiations to reach the implementing "123" agreement. The difficulties at this near-final stage raised doubts over the two states' ultimate acceptance of the 2005 nuclear agreement, and while a major formal hurdle has been passed a number of political challenges remain to be met before the deal can produce the results its supporters seek. But debate over consequences of these initiatives transcends the fate of US-India negotiations, for the nuclear deal has already impacted the rules of the nonproliferation order.

Two months after the initial US-India announcement, Canada announced its intention to seek nuclear engagement with India. But details about co-operative arrangements between these two countries have yet to be developed, in part hinging on the disposition of the US-India compact. Meanwhile, Canada's particular historical connection to India's nuclear program adds extra wrinkles to current policy debates. Canadian policy-makers face the daunting task of adjusting to the new realities created by the US initiative while sustaining longstanding non-proliferation, arms control and disarmament goals in the context of Canada's unique past and present relationship to India.

In November 2005, the Simons Centre for Non-Proliferation and Disarmament Research organized a two-day conference, attended by Canadian, Indian and US analysts, to consider the primary implications of the initial nuclear agreement.[1] Over the last year, the debate over the India-US agreement shifted from basic questions of its immediate import

---

[1] Proceedings of the conference and other analysis are available in Wade L. Huntley and Karthika Sasikumar, eds., *Nuclear Co-operation with India: New Challenges, New Opportunities.* This volume is available in print through major booksellers and as a PDF download at http://www.ligi.ubc.ca/admin/Centres/711/Nuclear_Cooperation_with_India.pdf.

and merit to, on the one hand, more nuanced questions about the details of arrangements being worked out by US and Indian negotiators and, on the other hand, to broader questions about the implications for the nonproliferation regime and for other countries with global interests.

To consider these questions, with particular attention to Canadian policy choices, the Simons Centre convened a second conference, "Canadian Policy on Nuclear Co-operation with India: Confronting New Dilemmas," in Ottawa on 19-20 March 2007. This publication presents revised versions of the papers presented at the conference and summarized below.

The conference's initial presentations and subsequent discussions were guided by a summary of developments and Canadian policy challenges provided by Michael Blackmore, Senior Policy Officer at the Nuclear Nonproliferation and Disarmament Division of DFAIT. The summary (included in this volume) included a list of fifteen questions particularly relevant to the policy-making process that participants sought, directly and indirectly, to address.

First, the conference attempted to locate the nuclear relationship within the context of the broader India-Canada relationship and its historical antecedents. As is well known, India's nuclear program was developed utilizing nuclear power reactors and technology provided by Canada. When, in 1974, India tested a nuclear device, calling it a "Peaceful Nuclear Explosion" (PNE), many Canadians felt India had broken promises that its nuclear program would be used solely for peaceful purposes. This perception has since shaped the bilateral relationship.

Ryan Touhey's contribution brought out the background of this troubled relationship, focusing on lessons from the transfer of Canadian atomic technology to India in the 1950s and 1960s. The proposed transfer of an NRX reactor to India under the auspices of the Colombo Plan was enthusiastically endorsed by senior Canadian officials in March 1955, but by 1963 the Canadian government began to suspect that New Delhi was not wholly committed to the ideal of "peaceful purposes." Nonetheless, Ottawa continued to sell reactors, fearing that not doing so would alienate New Delhi (India still remained the most likely partner for Canada in Asia) and that Canada could lose its niche in the Indian market to a competitor like France. Canada's failure to put into place mechanisms to evaluate the nuclear intentions of the Indian government on a continuous basis was partly responsible for the shock many policy-makers felt after India's 1974 test explosion.

Ashok Kapur's presentation picked up on the perceptual side of these difficulties. His assessment pointed to the fallacious basis of the "special relationship" that India and Canada claimed to have in the 1950s; in fact the two countries had quite antithetical interests when it came to nuclear issues. Indian officials did not see a fundamental incompatibility between development and security concerns. Whereas Canadians considered a PNE to be an oxymoronic term, most Indians saw the PNE as a way to convey to the world the capability and intention of the country to maintain a rudimentary nuclear deterrent, without flagrant defiance of the emerging norms against nuclear diffusion. For Kapur, Indians appropriately prioritized strategic needs over non-proliferation ideals, and saw the relationship with Canada as one to be manipulated as much as possible, without actually breaking formal laws or agreements, in order to secure the West's closely guarded atomic resources for their national program.

Cognizant of this historical context, the conference then examined the broader dimensions of India's current and future interest in developing its nuclear program.

Ravi Seethapathy's contribution assessed the contribution of nuclear energy to India's long-term energy security. His analysis showed that nuclear energy is a crucial component of energy planning for the Indian government. Nuclear power plants currently generate only 3 percent of the country's total electricity supply. For the next three decades, the demand for energy will rise by approximately 6 percent annually; with its current mix of energy sources, India's annual carbon emissions, currently the world's fifth largest, could triple. Seethapathy observed that, while the Indian government's plan includes increasing use of some alternative energy sources like wind and biofuel, the option with the lowest environmental impact would include greater reliance on nuclear power.

R. Rajaraman took up similar questions regarding India's nuclear weapons program and security interests. Rajaraman noted that India would have the potential to augment its arsenal of plutonium-based warheads by reprocessing spent, externally-supplied, uranium fuel. However, he also pointed out that India already has a sizable stockpile of 500 kilograms (kg) of weapons-grade plutonium from the CIRUS and Dhruva reactors—equivalent to about 100 nuclear weapons. In addition, the fast breeder reactors, if operational after 2010 as planned, would produce 135 kg of plutonium a year (30 weapons a year). This supply would be more than adequate for the limited number of nuclear warheads needed to implement India's stated doctrine of minimum nuclear deterrence. On this basis, Rajaraman questioned the common claim that nuclear co-operation will allow India to expand its nuclear arsenal by relieving civilian demand on India's limited indigenous uranium supplies.

The conference next turned to the international context. Two presentations squarely took on the question of the NPT's centrality in non-proliferation and the question of India's status in the global nuclear order.

James Keeley examined the political, legal and psychological implications of the "recognition" of India's nuclear status implicit in the nuclear deal. Keeley suggested that, just as the People's Republic of China had been a "big empty spot" on the maps of the US before its formal recognition, India's nuclear status also has to be acknowledged in some way by the major powers to close a gap in the global nuclear order. Keeley proposed rising above the NPT's binary categorization of countries into NWS and NNWS on the basis of a cutoff date in 1967, suggesting that nuclear-armed states outside of the NPT be termed States with Nuclear Weapons (SNW). States in this *sui generis* category would be treated differently, based on their behavior. The SNW category would allow the more responsible nuclear possessors like India to become stakeholders in the nonproliferation order without necessitating the Herculean task of amending the NPT.

Ernie Regehr's contribution focused on the possibility that India's search for legitimation could be harnessed to oblige it to accept some of the responsibilities of the NPT's recognized NWS. Regehr agreed with Keeley that there is value inherent in the term NWS that attracts India to the label, and also called for a new category he termed *De facto* NWS (DNWS). Such status would entail India accepting all the obligations that other NWS have accepted in the non-proliferation regime. Regehr listed ten NWS commitments to arms control and disarmament inherent in the NPT and assessed the status of India's adherence to them, concluding that presently India's declared commitments fall short on half of these measures. Regehr concluded that any Canadian civilian nuclear co-operation with India should first require full Indian acceptance of disarmament commitments, equivalent to those that NWS made through the NPT process. He noted that that the NWS's shortcomings in fulfilling their commitments in practice do not diminish their obligations, and so create no excuse for compromising expectations for India's own commitments.

The conference then considered broader international implications, including both the impact of nuclear co-operation with India on the norms and principles of the nuclear non-proliferation regime and the wider role of that regime in twenty-first century global security relations.

David Mutimer's analysis assessed the issue of nuclear co-operation with India within the framework of global norms. His presentation adopted the metaphor of "bullying" to examine the interaction between the US and India, from the negotiation of the NPT in the 1960s to the recent agreement on civil nuclear cooperation, noting how treating this interaction as a "social relationship" illuminates its power dynamics. Mutimer painted a picture of India as a classic victim of bullying, trying to acquire power by lashing out while accepting the power imbalance. Mutimer termed both the NPT's attempt to subject India to social isolation after 1968 and India's effort to break out of this prison with an explosive act in 1998 "world order moments". Thus, India's nuclear tests were the products of its relations with the US rather than with the stated targets of its nuclear weapons program —China and Pakistan. Mutimer clarified that his use of the bullying metaphor was not meant to elicit sympathy for India as a "victim" but simply to illustrate the power relationship in its dealings with the US. Mutimer provocatively raised the issue of Canadian responsibility, claiming that progress would not be achieved unless Canada interrogated its own role as an "enabler" of US power and bullying.

From a complementary vantage point, T.V. Paul's presentation applied "power transition theory" to argue that the non-proliferation regime is presently unable to accommodate rising powers such as India. Accounting for this changing power balance now necessitates adjusting the regime accordingly. Like Mutimer, Paul claimed that India had been victimized in the past because of its "bad timing" on nuclear issues, and, like Keeley, he compared the American recognition of India to its acceptance of Communist China in the 1970s. Paul predicted that frustrating India's quest to remedy the "status discrepancy" relative to the non-proliferation regime would lead to violent outcomes. He argued that nuclear co-operation with India would in fact strengthen the non-proliferation regime's service to long run strategic stability by giving India, a rising power, an incentive to cooperate with regime initiatives. Thus, Paul defended the Bush Administration's motivation to build up India's strategic capabilities against an emerging China. Paul concluded that Canada now has an opportunity to build better relations with India if it can change its "immature" attitude on the nuclear issue.

Stephen Schwartz commented on the discussions of the previous sessions from a global perspective. Evaluating the performance of the current nonproliferation regime, Schwartz noted that the number of nuclear warheads on the planet has decreased from 70,000 in 1987 to approximately 27,000 today, and that the NPT is the most signed treaty in history. Thus, it would be unfair to conclude that the global non-proliferation regime has failed. This context illuminates the main points of the previous presentations: there have been missed opportunities with regard to Canada's relationship with India, and inattention to warning signs on the nuclear issue. There have been competing priorities in foreign policy and nonproliferation has not always been on top of the agenda. Schwartz urged the global community to learn from this history and avoid repeating the mistakes of the Atoms for Peace plan. New nuclear co-operation with India would have global and regional implications—it cannot be a one-off event. Hence, Schwartz recommended that we should build onto the current regime, not around it. While India has been victimized in the past, two wrongs don't make a right. Safeguards are not incompatible with either India's military or nuclear energy interests. He claimed that other countries are not in the mood to accept the India-US deal as a *fait accompli* and an improved deal can still be worked out, that would also serve as a model for integrating other states into the system.

The editors' conclusion, developed on the basis of the conference presentations and discussions, conveys observations concerning the merits of nuclear co-operation with India, impacts on future directions for the non-proliferation regime, and implications for Canadian policy-making. This conclusion reflects the editors' own concerns and judgments; although it addresses the core questions animating the conference, it is not a consensus statement on behalf of the conference participants.

Canada and the US-India Civil Nuclear Co-operation Initiative: Issues for Consideration

Michael Blackmore[1]

On January 18, 2005 US President George Bush and Indian Prime Minister Manmohan Singh issued a joint declaration in which the US undertook to work domestically and with its international partners to achieve full civil nuclear cooperation with India, while India for its part committed to assume certain responsibilities related to non-proliferation. The statement was a landmark in that it signalled the intention of the US and India to work together to end the latter's more than thirty years of international isolation in terms of civilian nuclear cooperation.

Since that announcement the US-India civil nuclear cooperation initiative has moved forward on several tracks. In March 2006, India and the US reached agreement on a plan to separate India's civilian and military nuclear programmes, with the former to be placed voluntarily under IAEA safeguards. India has also begun to engage members of the NSG, both collectively (on the margins of the NSG Consultative Group meeting in October 2006) as well as individually, to solicit support for the necessary exemption from its Guidelines for transfers of nuclear and dual use items. Additionally, India has, however tentatively, initiated preliminary discussions with the IAEA on an 'India-specific' safeguards agreement for its civilian nuclear programme. The US and India have also engaged in negotiations on a bilateral nuclear cooperation agreement (so-called '123 agreement').

The most significant development to date, however, has been the adoption by the US Congress and subsequent signing into law in December 2006 of the Henry J. Hyde United States-India Peaceful Atomic Energy Cooperation Act of 2006. The Hyde Act, which was passed with strong bi-partisan support in both chambers of Congress, essentially establishes a waiver specific to India (contingent on certain Presidential determinations) from a long-standing requirement under American non-proliferation law that NNWS be subject to full-scope

---

[1] The views expressed in this paper are the author's alone and do not necessarily reflect the position of the Department of Foreign Affairs and International Trade (DFAIT).

IAEA safeguards to be eligible for bilateral nuclear cooperation with the US. This waiver now allows the US to conclude the '123 agreement'.

Several steps remain, however, before the US-India initiative can be realized. The US and India must complete negotiations on the '123 agreement', where public indications suggest there may be several outstanding issues to resolve. Additionally, India must complete negotiations with the IAEA on a non-confirming (i.e. 'India-specific') safeguards agreement to cover its declared civilian nuclear programme. That agreement, once completed, may also have to be approved by the Agency's Board of Governors given that it is unlikely to conform to either of the Agency's model safeguards arrangements. The Board will wish to ensure that any new type of safeguards agreement does not diminish the reputation of the Agency or undermine its safeguards system. The 45-member NSG, of which Canada is a member, will then have to decide whether or not to approve an exemption for India from its Guidelines. Similar considerations and concerns will likely pre-occupy NSG governments. Only once these processes have been completed can the Administration submit a US-India bilateral nuclear cooperation agreement to both chambers of Congress for an up or down vote.

The timing of the unfolding of this complicated multi-track process remains unclear. Assuming, however, that the United States and India are able to conclude a '123 agreement' and India is able to complete safeguards negotiations with the IAEA, Canada and other NSG members will at some future point in time have to decide whether or not to support an exemption for India from the NSG Guidelines and effectively end India's more than three decades of isolation from international nuclear co-operation. In the process policy-makers will need to carefully weigh a variety of important factors and interests before making a final determination, not the least of which is whether or not this initiative makes a net contribution to nuclear non-proliferation.

This process will be particularly sensitive for Canada given our difficult nuclear history with India. As is well-known, India used plutonium derived from a research reactor (CIRUS) supplied by Canada under the Colombo Plan in the 1950s, despite a peaceful uses assurance on India's part, to produce the nuclear explosive device which it tested in 1974. It was that mis-appropriation of nuclear technology supplied for peaceful purposes that subsequently led to the promulgation of Canadian non-proliferation policy, as articulated in Cabinet directives in 1974 and 1976 and reaffirmed by the Standing Committee on Foreign Affairs and International Trade (SCFAIT) in 1999, as well as to the development of the broader international nuclear export control regime, including the NSG itself.

This conference presents a timely opportunity for consideration of several issues which could help to inform the policy process. Conference participants might, for example, help to inform the policy-making process by addressing the following questions:

1. How might a decision to grant India an exemption from the NSG Guidelines be expected to impact the broader nuclear non-proliferation, arms control and disarmament regime? What, if any, affect could a decision to grant India an exemption be expected to have on our efforts to stem the proliferation of weapons of mass destruction and to deal with states of proliferation concern?

2. What options might NSG Participating Governments consider in order to strengthen the non-proliferation elements of the US-India initiative should the NSG ultimately agree to grant India and exemption from its Guidelines? Are there criteria which the NSG might establish for nuclear co-operation with India which would help to ensure that the initiative represents a net gain for the nuclear non-proliferation regime? Are there conditionalities in the Hyde Act which might be adopted in an NSG exemption?

3. Should the NSG agree to an exemption for India from its Guidelines, how could Canada's own national non-proliferation policy be adjusted to account for this new reality?

4. Given its stated 'redlines', what further commitments can realistically be sought of India to move it closer to the international nuclear non-proliferation mainstream?

5. How can India's desire to reserve the right to 'corrective measures' in the event of an interruption in fuel supply to safeguarded reactors be reconciled with the requirement for it to place its civilian nuclear facilities and materials under safeguards in perpetuity?

6. In the July 18, 2005 joint declaration India undertook to work with the US for the conclusion of a multilateral FMCT. In the Conference on Disarmament and UNGA First Committee, however, India has indicated that it could only accept an "effectively verifiable" FMCT which would seem contrary to the current US position. How will these differences in approach be reconciled by the two parties. How could Canada best engage India bilaterally on FMCT issues?

7. Is there margin for further strengthening the Indian separation plan, particularly with regard to India's plans for breeder reactors? Why will they be excluded if they are intended for civilian power production?

8. There has been extensive debate on the issue of whether or not allowing India to import uranium for use in safeguarded reactors would free up India's limited domestic uranium supply for its strategic programme. What is the assessment of participants on the impact an NSG exemption for India would have on India's nuclear weapons capability?

9. What is the probable impact of an India-specific exemption for regional stability?

10. What implications might Canada's eventual decision on an NSG exemption for India have on our bilateral relationship with the US?

11. What implications might Canada's decision have for our broader relationship with India?

12. To what degree, if any, can it be expected that India will re-align its foreign policy with US (and more broadly Western) interests if accorded civil nuclear cooperation?

13. Pakistan has raised concerns that an India-specific exemption from the NSG Guidelines would be discriminatory and has suggested rather a criteria-based approach to an exemption that would be applicable to all states which have not signed the NPT. How might NSG members, including Canada, respond to Pakistan's desire for equal treatment?

14. Public debate in India has revealed considerable opposition to the US-India initiative, in particular from the nuclear scientific establishment and from left-wing political parties. What are the prospects, if any, that the Indian government will not be able to overcome this domestic opposition to the accord? To what degree will the domestic political schedules in both India and the US determine the window of opportunity for completing a deal?

15. How important is the outcome of the US-India initiative in terms of India's economic growth and in terms of environmental sustainability?

Troubled from the beginning: Canada's nuclear relations with India during the 1960s

Ryan Touhey

In May 1974, the Indian government tested what it called a "peaceful nuclear device." The decision to do so sparked a viscerally bitter reaction from Ottawa, as it was widely suspected that the plutonium used in the device had been extracted from the donated Canada-India Reactor (CIR) despite a bilateral understanding that the reactor would be used solely for peaceful purposes. This event led to a prolonged cooling-off period between the two countries; moreover, it has clouded the fact that Canada's historic nuclear relationship with India has been plagued by differences over the role of international safeguards and the efficacy of the NPT that the Indians viewed with scepticism. Within months of Ottawa's decision in 1955 to donate a Canadian reactor to India, both countries were at odds over the question of the application of international safeguards to the Canadian reactor.

Differences over safeguards lingered well into the final round of negotiations for two further CANDU nuclear reactor sales in 1963 and 1966. After accepting watered-down safeguards for the CIR in late 1959, Ottawa was forced to play "catch-up" on the question of safeguards in its future dealings with the Indians. In addition, Canadian politicians and policy-makers in the Department of External Affairs (DEA) became increasingly suspicious of the motives of the Indian nuclear program, fearing that New Delhi might use Canadian technology to develop nuclear weapons. The final reactor sale was approved in December 1966, just as Ottawa and New Delhi were disagreeing on the merits of the proposed NPT (that was finalized in 1968). Nuclear co-operation between both countries had marked one of the last substantive links in a bilateral relationship that had become strained due to diverging responses to the Cold War, and the advent of new leadership in both countries. India and Canada interpreted the issue of nuclear proliferation in terms far different than anyone would have expected years earlier. By virtue of their different interpretations over nuclear safeguards and nuclear proliferation, the Canadian government was frequently forced to react to Indian policies, leaving Ottawa with little ability to influence New Delhi when it sought to do so.

In March 1955, Prime Minister Louis St. Laurent's cabinet approved a proposal to offer the Indian government a Canadian-designed NRX experimental reactor through the Colombo Plan. The reasoning behind this was twofold. First, Ottawa believed that such a move was of considerable international political importance for the West in its attempts to secure the loyalty of the developing world as the Cold War heated up. Second, there were economic advantages for the St. Laurent government. It was argued that, since Canada was not a nuclear power, "most Asian countries would find it less difficult and embarrassing to receive direct assistance from us [Canada]…than from either of the larger atomic powers whose motives might be suspect." A cabinet memorandum concluded that Canadian business and the atomic industry could gain a competitive advantage in an emerging field and Ottawa could actively assist "their position for constructing various types of atomic units in Canada or abroad in later years."[1] India was seen as the logical choice: it had a developing atomic energy infrastructure and the two other major recipients of Canadian Colombo Plan aid were Ceylon and Pakistan. Ceylon's need for such a reactor at the time was limited and Pakistan was politically unstable—its leaders did not have the prestige in Ottawa that India's Prime Minister Jawaharlal Nehru enjoyed.[2]

Many in Ottawa thought the reactor transfer would be a simple arrangement; instead, it became mired in lengthy negotiations as the Indians pressed for a more advanced reactor than the NRX and then as differences arose over the question of effective safeguards for the NRX and its uranium fuel rods. Only after Ottawa increased its Colombo Plan funding to India and firmly told the Indians that the only reactor on the table was the NRX did Nehru and his chief atomic scientist, Homi J. Bhabha, accept Ottawa's offer. On September 16, 1955, Ottawa and New Delhi jointly announced the project that became known as the CIR. The negotiations that led to the transfer of the reactor proved to be the easy part. By comparison, the ensuing negotiations concerning the control and

---

[1] LAC, RG 25 Vol. 9551, File 8-A-India-2-1970/1. See Memorandum to Cabinet, March 29, 1955, Subject: "Atomic Energy and Canada's Colombo Plan Contribution."
[2] For a history of Canada's foreign relations with India see Ryan Touhey, "Dealing with the peacock: India in Canadian foreign relations, 1941–1976." Ph.D. dissertation (University of Waterloo, 2006). The decision and subsequent negotiations that led to Ottawa transferring the NRX to India is superbly dealt with by Greg Donaghy in "Nehru's Reactor: The Origins of Indo-Canadian Nuclear Cooperation, 1955–59" in Canada's Global Engagements and Relations with India, ed. by Christopher Raj and Abdul Nafey (New Delhi: Manak Publications, 2007).

use of the plutonium created by the NRX proved to be a lingering headache for Indo-Canadian relations. Ottawa soon learned that it had a far different view than did New Delhi on the interpretation of safeguards. No international guidelines or regulatory body yet existed that provided set rules and procedures on the handling and use of plutonium. The NRX reactor could produce enough plutonium to make several atomic weapons, and Canada was planning to provide the necessary fuel elements.

The differences on plutonium safeguards were apparent as Canadian officials met with their Indian counterparts in late 1955. Secretary of State for External Affairs (SSEA) Lester Pearson and Canadian High Commissioner Escott Reid hoped to finalize the question of safeguards; instead, Nehru shrewdly let Bhabha negotiate with Pearson and Reid, who both later admitted in correspondence to the DEA to having been out of their depth in the discussion. The two Canadians pressed Bhabha to accept safeguards on who would control the fuel for the reactor and the subsequent plutonium created by the spent fuel; however, Bhabha demurred, countering that the Indians could be trusted to monitor the plutonium on their own without accepting IAEA safeguards which, like the agency, were still in their infancy. Bhabha suggested that given the difficulty in reaching a consensus on the reactor fuel, it was perhaps best to avoid mentioning any arrangements for fuel in any prospective agreement. Bhabha's logic was based on the fact that fuel would not be needed until the project was near completion, which was expected to be in two years' time (but turned out to be over four). Also, because the agreement would not discuss any fuel arrangement it could not, technically, violate or establish any precedent that would affect the regulations or statutes of the proposed international atomic energy agency. Pearson's diary entry indicated that Bhabha provided assurances that the final details should meet regulations adopted by the IAEA. Reid's account of the conversation differs, however, suggesting Bhabha remained inflexible on controls. In particular, Bhabha disagreed, notably over what powers the IAEA would possess. The course of events that followed confirms that Reid's account was correct. Nonetheless, Pearson was left satisfied enough with the talks that upon return to Ottawa he agreed that construction on the reactor should not be delayed any further; Cabinet approved the deal on December 7, 1955 (Touhey 2006).

On April 28, 1956, Nehru and Reid formally signed the NRX reactor agreement in New Delhi, but questions concerning the application of IAEA safeguards, inspections, and the sale of uranium to India remained unsettled for the next three years as both sides entered into a series of protracted discussions. After a final round of increasingly tense discussions, both sides agreed in November 1959 on watered-down safeguards for the CIR, but the arrangement was kept secret (Donaghy 2007). The new-found Indian flexibility does not appear to have risen from any great epiphany on the benefit of safeguards. Instead, Bhabha likely overestimated the number of quality uranium rods the Indians could produce: Canadian sources suspected that the Indians had produced one by the early fall of 1959, while the CIR required 192 to act at full capacity.

For the time being the problems were solved. The CIR was the only Canadian-designed reactor operating in a foreign market and AECL, with the support of the DEA, hoped that this would cultivate new clients and generate further sales. It did. No sooner had the CIR gone critical than Bhabha, with Nehru's support, in the summer of 1962 expressed interest in a new advanced Canadian product, the CANDU nuclear reactor. This time, discussed below, the DEA adopted a more resolute approach over the question on safeguards, but Ottawa was willing, pushed along by the exuberant lobbying of AECL, to continue the potentially lucrative sale of reactors to India. In 1963, the newly elected Pearson government agreed to continue negotiations with New Delhi, initiated by the Progressive Conservatives, for a Canadian-designed Heavy Water reactor to be constructed in Rajasthan. As in the case of the agreement concerning the CIR reactor, the negotiations for the Rajasthan reactor were arduous as Ottawa pushed for stricter safeguards.

In the years following the CIR agreement, Ottawa had become a key international supporter for nuclear safeguards whereas Bhabha remained effusive in his disdain for them. In March 1959, Canada helped form the "Ottawa Group" to support safeguards in the IAEA. Secretary of State for External Affairs Howard Green was a passionate proponent of nuclear disarmament, and many of his officials within the DEA—one being Norman Robertson—supported his zeal on this issue. Able to refer to the IAEA framework that had not existed in 1955, Ottawa proved in this second round of negotiations to be far more assertive in its demands regarding safeguards. Still, both sides were pursuing complementary objectives. The Indians needed the technology, a number of Canadians wanted to sell them the technology, and dollars trumped security concerns. Negotiations continued and Nehru announced in the Lok Sabha in August 1962 his government's formal interest in building a Canadian-designed Heavy Water reactor in Rajasthan. Historian Robert Bothwell has suggested that throughout this process the DEA adopted a far more hard-line approach over the question of safeguards than did AECL, which was motivated by sales and the subtle Indian threat that if they did not buy from Canada, they would from someone else (Bothwell 1988).

Once the Liberals were re-elected, Bhabha travelled to Ottawa in May 1963 to lobby Ottawa; however, DEA officials had begun to question Bhabha's ambitions for the Indian nuclear program and were uncertain to what extent India's nuclear intentions were strictly for peaceful purposes. These doubts increased after the Sino-Indian border war in the autumn of 1962. Chester Ronning, the Canadian high commissioner to New Delhi, harboured doubts regarding India's nuclear ambitions but cautiously supported the Indian request on the basis of his expectations that the Indians would not divert from peaceful purposes "at least until after [the] Chinese have announced their intention or demonstrated capacity to explode [a] nuclear device." Ronning's despatch, however, has overtones of Shakespeare's Hamlet. While India "firmly intends to use [sic] CANDU-Reactor for peaceful purposes only and will abide by peaceful intent of the agreement," he added another caveat: "I admit I was somewhat disturbed by my conversations with Bhabha and Khera and it is only after much soul-searching I have reached [the] conclusion we should go ahead with project." [3]

Despite his shaky support, Ronning advised that it was likely that Ottawa would have to continue to press the Indians to accept IAEA safeguards. Ronning suggested two alternatives if Indian cooperation was not forthcoming:

> (a) insist upon obtaining completely satisfactory agreement from Indians in hope of preventing any possible use of our equipment for war purposes, or (b) accept flexibility involved in present Indian draft that may risk possibility of Indians using fissionable material from their fuel for non-peaceful purposes.

He advised that if pressed, Ottawa should choose the second alternative, fearing that too rigid an agreement might lead the Indians to violate it entirely if faced by grave threats to national security. Such a case would "have [a] very bad effect upon our relations with India—especially after such lengthy negotiations." Besides, Ronning added, if the Indians ultimately chose to use their own fissionable material, the second option would allow "us to close our eyes to eventual disposition of that material

---

[3] LAC, RG 25 Vol. 5034, File 1617-40 pt. 5, Ronning to DEA, Despatch No. 776, July 26, 1963. This was circulated to the Privy Council Office also. Khera was an influential cabinet secretary in Nehru's government.

particularly if at that time we are not prepared publicly to endorse possible change in India's present attitude and intent." Realistically, if the Indians violated the agreement and used their own fuel for nuclear weapons, there would be little Ottawa could do to stop them short of cutting further nuclear assistance. On the other hand, Ronning added that some solace might be taken from the fact that it would be at least five years before the reactor would become operational, and in the initial stages much of the nuclear material would be subject to full safeguards. Ultimately, Ronning was doubtful that Ottawa could get much more from the Indians, and Ottawa's harder line appeared to have reaped some gains.

The Indians had given Canada the "right to inspect and verify disposition of product Canadian fuel, right to inspect premises of reactor plant, right to obtain records of all fuel used in reactor and guarantee of prior notification of disposition of product of nuclear fuel." This was more than Ronning thought Bhabha would ever allow considering he was initially determined "to give us even less than provided by CIR agreement." Finally, he added, if the Indians did not get the reactor from Ottawa, they would get it from somewhere else, and "these considerations lead me to conclusion that we should come to an early decision in favour of CANDU reactor in India whether or not we obtain further concessions from Bhabha."[4]

Norman Robertson, the under-secretary of state for external affairs (USSEA), suspected that further concessions could be wrung from Bhabha. He was right. The recently signed PTBT and domestic debate over nuclear missiles for the Canadian armed forces had heightened public attention at home and elsewhere on Canada's atomic co-operation with India. Robertson noted that "there has already been press and radio comments to the effect that Canada has put India in a substantially improved position to build a bomb if they so desire." It was imperative that if Canada was going to sign the PTBT, its position on safeguards should reflect the "spirit of the Test Ban Agreement and our determination to avoid, to the extent we have influence, the extension of nuclear military capability. It would follow therefore that we must continue to seek adequate safeguards."[5] Robertson advised that if the Indians were willing to be flexible on issues such as verifying the disposition of nuclear fuel and other audit procedures, Ottawa could soothe Indian feelings and permit the Indians reciprocity so they could in turn inspect a similar Canadian reactor. While "we had never anticipated

---

4 Ibid.
5 Ibid., Robertson to Ronning, Despatch No. E-1273, 29 July 1963.

that we could prevent the Indians from breaking or violating the agreement," Ottawa was not asking Bhabha to accept anything more than the "rights" Ronning had outlined. Robertson informed Ronning that both sides were close to reaching an agreement but the ball was in Bhabha's court. The DEA was willing to send the deal to cabinet provided it could assure the government that the agreement provided reasonable safeguards and was consistent in following Canada's views toward limiting military nuclear proliferation.[6]

Bhabha grudgingly relented. On November 21, the Canadian cabinet agreed to the deal, noting "negotiations have been successfully completed between India covering all aspects of cooperation between the two countries in the construction of the Rajasthan Atomic Power Station." Canada would provide technical information and financing for the purchase of Canadian-supplied material, equipment, and fuel. Agreements ensured that the Rajasthan station would be partnered with a Canadian reactor at Douglas Point, Ontario. Both stations were to be used only for peaceful purposes.[7]

The Canadians basked in what appeared to be a superb deal for Canada. AECL strengthened its relationship with India and proved that a small country like Canada could carve out a niche for itself on the world nuclear market. Indeed, the SSEA, Paul Martin, suggested in cabinet that "the success of the negotiations on the safeguards provisions made possible a major programme of collaboration going beyond the establishment of the CANDU power station."[8] DEA officials could be pleased with having negotiated a deal that not only respected their desire for safeguards but also forced the Indians to compromise from their earlier position. Unlike the CIR deal, this had some teeth to it. For their part, the Indians had made a concession that they could apparently tolerate. The deal ensured nuclear co-operation and guaranteed them the receipt of the advanced Canadian technology.

The Indians sought to rapidly purchase another CANDU reactor to be labelled the RAPP II, but in the interim, profound changes had occurred in New Delhi. Nehru died in May 1964 and was replaced by his Congress party colleague Lal Bahadur Shastri. Nehru and Bhabha had worked

---

[6] LAC, RG 25 Vol. 5034, File 1617-40 pt. 5 Robertson to Ronning, Despatch No. E-1273, July 29, 1963

[7] LAC, RG 25 Vol. 10049, File 20-1-2 India pt. 1.1, P.C. 1963–1725, November 21, 1963. See also Memorandum from O.G. Stoner to DEA Legal Division, December 5, 1963. In particular, articles VIII, IX, X, XI, XII, XIIII, XIV, and XV suggest that the Canadians had extracted significant concessions from the Indians.

[8] LAC, RG 2 Vol. 6254, Cabinet Minutes, November 14, 1963.

closely together for fifteen years in shaping the Indian nuclear program. Unlike his Cambridge-educated and worldly predecessor, Shastri had barely travelled outside India's borders and knew little about India's nuclear program until becoming prime minister. On June 10, 1965, Shastri travelled to Canada for his first and only meeting with Canadian officials. As the Canadians prepared for the visit, Pearson agreed with the recommendation of the DEA's deputy under-secretary, A.E. Ritchie, who highlighted nuclear proliferation as one of the key topics that should be delicately discussed. Ritchie's recommendations were as follows:

> (a) the continuation of India's policy of abstaining from a nuclear weapons programme with emphasis on your June 3 statement on uranium policy and bearing in mind reports of Indian preparations for a "peaceful" explosion; (b) the situation in Vietnam viewed broadly and from the viewpoint of the Commission; (c) China's objectives, especially in Southeast Asia. In turn we can expect Mr. Shastri to focus attention on certain Indian problems, including: (a) the difficultly of financing India's fourth Five-year Plan, no doubt referring to the sympathetic reception his representations received in Moscow last month; (b) the Chinese problem as seen from New Delhi; and perhaps (c) relations with Pakistan. [9]

In the months preceding the Shastri visit, informal exchanges had taken place between Bhabha and Lorne Gray, the president of AECL, and financing discussions on a second CANDU reactor were likely once the Indians made their intentions official. Bhabha had informally signalled that India might not be willing to agree to the same safeguard agreements that defined the RAPP I agreement, implying that they were too rigorous for New Delhi's liking. Ottawa's long-term objective was to have all the Canadian reactors placed under IAEA inspections. Concurrently, the government was moving toward applying stricter safeguards on uranium fuel. Cabinet sought to prohibit the export of Canadian uranium to any country that might use it for non-peaceful purposes. While Pearson and Martin had Shastri's ear, they were urged "to impress upon him our hope and expectation that the two Governments will act upon the foregoing article and that eventually Canadian-Indian safeguards problems will be resolved entirely within an IAEA framework."[10]

---

[9] LAC, Pearson Papers, MG 26 N3 Vol. 269, File 818.1/I39, Shastri Conf., Memorandum for the Prime Minister/Paul Martin by A.E. Ritchie, June 4, 1965.
[10] LAC, RG 25 Vol. 3494, File 18-1-H-IND-1965/1, Visit of Prime Minister Shastri of India, Briefing Book.

During the meetings, both sides exchanged papers outlining their views on global non-proliferation and clearly the Indians were confident, perhaps overly so at the time, about their nuclear capabilities. Shastri informed his interlocutors that India was a nuclear power and a good deal of domestic public opinion favoured nuclear weapons for India. New Delhi had a nuclear capability but the government "had taken a categorically clear stand that its policy was not to make nuclear weapons. He hoped they could stick to it." The Indian leader encouraged Ottawa to work with New Delhi to produce "substantial results" in the elimination of nuclear weapons.[11]

A closer look reveals some bewildering decisions on the part of Canadian policy-makers, particularly Paul Martin. In his memoirs, Martin claims that since meeting Homi Bhabha at the United Nations in the mid-1950s, he had "realized that he [Bhabha] intended India to produce its own atomic bomb (Martin 1985). This was certainly not Nehru's position, nor that of his successor, Lal Bahadur Shastri". Martin's recollection of Bhabha's intentions is misleading. If Martin truly knew about Bhabha's ambitions, there is no evidence that he went to cabinet with them during the CIR negotiations or afterward. Admittedly, he supported Norman Robertson's tough stance to secure appropriate safeguards on the RAPP I, but it appears that Nehru's stature as an international statesman led Pearson and Martin to pause before challenging the Indians, and Martin certainly did not object to the eventual sale of the RAPP I or its successor, the RAPP II, to India.

Moreover, the briefing book prepared for Pearson and Martin noted that while the majority of India's nuclear infrastructure was related to civilian objectives, a recently built plutonium separation plant raised eyebrows and India's geopolitical situation served as an additional red flag:

> The construction [of the plutonium separation plant] and recent completion of an industrial sized plutonium separation plant is difficult to reconcile with Indian requirements for a realistic civilian research and power programme over the next few years. The separation of plutonium is, however, a prime requisite for the development and production of nuclear weapons. In the absence heretofore of compelling military requirements for nuclear weapons, economic and political considerations, including the Nehru legacy of pacifist morality and aversion to nuclear weapons, have tended to deter India

---

[11] Ibid., Vol. 10417, File 27-20-5 pt. 2, DEA to CDN Embassy, Washington D.C., Despatch No. K146, June 16, 1965.

from embarking on a nuclear weapons programme. However, the threat to Indian security and prestige posed by Communist China, particularly since China has tested nuclear devices, could militate against these factors in increasing measure. The present and future development of India's civilian nuclear research and power programme will continue to ensure that a militarily significant scale in four to five years from now, could be initiated very quickly and without a prohibitive diversion of manpower resources. There is no evidence to date that a decision has or has not been taken by the Indian government to commence a nuclear weapons programme. It is known, nevertheless, that the operation of the Canada-India Reactor (CIR) at Trombay has been oriented towards optimizing the production of weapons-grade plutonium since the summer of 1963.[12]

Furthermore, the British defence minister, Denis Healey, told his Canadian counterpart, Paul Hellyer, that the Indians were "making all necessary preparations for a test explosion sometime before the end of the year, ostensibly in a form which could be justified as being for peaceful purposes."[13] This was faulty intelligence, yet the DEA, having no external intelligence capabilities of its own to rely on, believed that the British view was credible.[14] Any Indian nuclear explosion would have immense ramifications for Indo-Canadian relations as the plutonium would have to have been taken from the CIR, thus violating past Indian assurances.

Despite these cautions, the Pearson government continued to ponder ongoing nuclear assistance to India mainly because it believed that it had little room in which to manoeuvre. If Canada rebuffed further Indian requests for nuclear assistance, it risked aggravating the largest and most important democracy in Asia. It also risked jeopardizing a market for the Canadian nuclear industry, as well as other exports. There was no shortage

---

[12] LAC, RG 25 Vol. 3494, File 18-1-H-IND-1965/1, Visit of Prime Minister Shastri of India, Briefing Book.

[13] Ibid. The Americans believed that India could manufacture a bomb within one to three years after a decision to do so was made.

[14] In February 1965, John Starnes, the Canadian ambassador to West Germany and later the head of intelligence for the RCMP, attended a conference in Switzerland hosted by the International Institute for Strategic Studies on nuclear proliferation. Personal and informal talks during the conference left Starnes "with the distinct impression" that India had already decided to create a nuclear weapons programme. Whether he relayed his impressions to the DEA remains unclear. See John Starnes, *Closely Guarded: A Life in Canadian Security and Intelligence* (Toronto: University of Toronto Press, 1998), 107-108.

of Western countries, particularly France, that would eagerly replace Canada in the Indian nuclear market.

Just as important to the Canadian government in its nuclear co-operation with New Delhi was India's role in the non-proliferation discussions at the UN throughout 1966. Indira Gandhi, Nehru's daughter, was now at the helm of India's nuclear policy, having replaced Shastri, who passed away in February 1966. Less than two weeks into Gandhi's tenure, Bhabha perished in an airplane crash on the day she was officially sworn into office. Coincidentally, Bhabha was to have briefed her that same day on India's nuclear program, and it is unclear to what extent Indira Gandhi knew about the topic. Nevertheless, the tough-minded Gandhi was now responsible for choosing Bhabha's successor and for largely determining India's nuclear program.

In February 1966, the Indian representative to the NPT negotiations in Geneva, V.C. Trivedi, insisted that the nuclear weapons state "haves" treat the "have-nots" equitably and with mutual obligations. India, he asserted, wanted a treaty that obligated NWS and NNWS to stop production of nuclear weapons and any related delivery mechanisms (Perkovich 2001). This stance suggested that the Indians were moving away from Shastri's earlier hope that American and Soviet security assurances to India in its strained relationship with China would be enough to keep New Delhi from developing nuclear weapons.

Policy-makers within the Commonwealth and Disarmament divisions of DEA were skeptical that India would accept any agreement that restricted the right of non-nuclear nations to test a nuclear device. They also disagreed with a quickly scuttled American idea that Ottawa and Washington approach New Delhi and offer India a nuclear device for a "peaceful" explosion in light of the changing security environment in South Asia. In October 1964, China had stunned the Indians by detonating their first nuclear explosive device. This event automatically changed the balance of power in the region and was a blow to India's fragile sense of security in the immediate aftermath of the Chinese victory in the 1962 border war. Now that China had "gone nuclear" and acquired the "prestige" of being a member of an elite club, it was unlikely that Indians would accept "any such limitation on non-nuclear powers even if she has no intention of testing a nuclear device." A departmental memorandum weighed the pros and cons of acting with the Americans in lobbying India against testing a nuclear device. The analysis suggests the fragility of the Canadian position with doubts expressed as to Ottawa's ability to influence New Delhi.[15]

That Ottawa in just over ten years since deliberating whether to offer India an atomic reactor could find itself in such a vulnerable position, whereby it had "no real levers" is shocking. This dilemma, exacerbated by competing and conflicting governmental trade and non-proliferation interests, illustrates the naïveté with which Ottawa had been negotiating with India in what was frequently an ad hoc manner. The Indians had given Canada verbal and written assurances on both the CIR and RAPP I reactors and Shastri had apparently repeated the same assurances during his 1965 visit, but this obviously had not assuaged some officials in the DEA. On the other hand, A.G. Campbell, director of the Commonwealth division, argued that "a direct approach could be taken by India as an affront as we would be saying in effect we don't trust your previous pledges to us." Besides, he concluded that the Indians surely knew by now that Ottawa would react unfavourably on any nuclear explosion. This became a long-standing and utterly vapid assumption among some DEA policy-makers in analyzing bilateral nuclear co-operation. In the meantime, Ottawa would be wise to restate its position in "the negotiations over safeguards for RAPP II when these move from the technical to the political sphere."[16]

The negotiations for RAPP II continued throughout 1966, coinciding with the NPT discussions. However, talks with the Gandhi government on safeguards continued to be problematic. The Indians now sought to avoid Canadian safeguards "by procuring only the conventional parts of the reactor in Canada while making the rest in India," which was unacceptable in Canadian eyes (Bothwell 1988). When China tested a third nuclear device on May 9, the Indian parliament erupted into a stormy debate as the hawks attacked the inchoate government policy on whether India would develop its own nuclear weapons program. The response from the minister of external affairs, Swaran Singh, subtly suggests that the government was willing to listen to the hawks. Singh confirmed in the Lok Sabha that India would proceed "with development of nuclear energy

---

[15] LAC, RG 25 Vol. 10098, File 20-1-2 pt. 2, Memorandum from A.G. Campbell to Blair Seaborn, March 11, 1966.

[16] Ibid. Ottawa also had to worry about the Pakistani reaction. "Should India ever explode a nuclear device, even a 'peaceful' one, we could be in for a very difficult time from Pakistan. The Foreign Minister, Mr. Bhutto, has said that Pakistanis would 'eat grass' in an effort to build a nuclear device should India do so. At best, we could expect to be accused of favouring India and of having been duped by Indian perfidy as the Pakistanis had told us all along we would be. Almost certainly the reaction could be more violent than that."

for "non-peaceful purposes" unless there was progress in the direction of nuclear non-proliferation and a guarantee by the main nuclear powers to "all non-nuclear powers" against nuclear blackmail [*sic*]." Singh's comments were supported by Gandhi, with both agreeing that the "defence of our territorial integrity will be the paramount consideration guiding our policy in the field."[17] Yet their response also had a carefully phrased caveat that linked any decision as to the direction of the Indian nuclear program to the ongoing Geneva discussions. The answer contained something for everyone and suggests that Indian policy was in flux.

The question of whether India would manufacture a nuclear device was raised again in the Lok Sabha. Singh's response was less strident than that of May but it remained inconclusive:

> Successive Prime Ministers of India have repeatedly declared their determination not to manufacture a bomb. We want to harness the nuclear energy for peaceful purposes. But the world, especially the nuclear powers, should not take our self-abnegation as a part of our duty and their right. We should be assured of reasonable hope that an agreement on disarmament will be signed and signed soon. If the nuclear powers fail to agree to both non-dissemination and non-proliferation, India may be forced to reconsider her decision.[18]

These limited assurances also whipped up tension on the subcontinent. The Pakistani government increased its lobbying of Ottawa, urging against the reactor sale on the grounds that India was set to explode a nuclear device. The allegations came as the cabinet debate on the proposed sale of the third reactor began in Ottawa.

On July 27, the Pearson government agreed that Canada should finance the second phase of the Rajasthan Atomic Power Project provided that the Indians consented to appropriate safeguards as accorded to the RAPP I. But now Paul Martin wanted to press for more stringent safeguard requirements. He suspected that the Pakistani allegations were likely unfounded, informing Pearson that the "best intelligence assessment is that the Indians have no present intention to explode a 'peaceful' nuclear device." But he believed on principle that Ottawa must push India toward accepting IAEA safeguards. Pearson remained circumspect. He agreed

---

17 LAC, RG 20 Vol. 1672, File 3-51-1 pt. 2, "The Indiagram" Office of the High Commissioner for India #29/66, May 13, 1966.

18 Lok Sabha Debates, Question No. 877, August 1, 1966.

with his minister's desire but wrote on the memorandum: "How can we do this now—after having made other arrangements with India?"

Martin had three motivating reasons though for why Ottawa should press the Indians:

> a) we would substantially improve the chances of securing Pakistan's assent to the transfer to the IAEA of responsibility for safeguards administration; b) in the same connection, success with the Indians would provide an impressive Canadian answer to the Pakistani diplomatic offensive regarding the Indian potential for making nuclear weapons. c) We will never have a better lever to apply with the Indians than their present application for credit financing of RAPP II.[19]

Therefore, Martin recommended that Ottawa seek agreement from the Indians that at an appropriate time the IAEA would become responsible for the monitoring of safeguards, while strongly hinting that the financing was tied to a positive result. Martin was uncertain whether the Indians would go for this tough-love approach, but with the death of Bhabha he surmised that the chances of successfully reaching an agreement had improved. Pearson disagreed; he thought the chances of India making a nuclear bomb had "probably improved" and the Pakistani charges could not be ignored. He saw "little chance" of successfully linking the financing of the reactor to the IAEA safeguards and suggested that "if we persist now we are likely to get into serious trouble with India."

Martin's memorandum was generated in part from a letter Gandhi had sent Pearson in June. She had written Pearson hoping to exchange views on matters of bilateral interest and invited Pearson to visit India. Martin supported Gandhi's invitation, strongly hinting that Pearson should make the visit as "no Canadian Prime Minister has been in Asia since 1958 and visits of Canadian Cabinet Ministers have been few and far between."[20] Pearson declined the Indian invitation, citing a heavy schedule, but agreed with his minister that a response concentrating on Indochina and the commission problems, atomic energy, and development assistance should be sent.[21]

---

[19] LAC, Paul Martin Papers, MG 32 B 12 Vol. 225, File 225-4 Commonwealth 1965–67, Memorandum from Martin to Pearson, July 29, 1966.
[20] LAC, RG 25 Vol. 10098, File 20-1-2 India pt. 2, Memorandum from Martin to Pearson, July 11, 1966.
[21] Ibid., Pearson to Indira Gandhi, August 2, 1966.

Pearson's eventual letter to Gandhi stressed that Ottawa sought bilateral co-operation on the current Geneva NPT discussions and desired a "future role of IAEA in connection with the Rajasthan reactors as contemplated in the agreement of November 1963." Both countries, he added, had a chance to "contribute a great deal to our mutual efforts to strengthen the international safeguards system and to persuade certain other countries (of interest to us both) to accept the measures necessary to the attainment of this objective." Canada and India upheld an important role in a pivotal debate, he continued. Both nations had the technical ability to manufacture nuclear arms, "but we have chosen not to do so." The two must work together to prevent the spread of nuclear weapons, and co-operating on the NPT negotiations was a tangible means of doing so.[22]

The Indians, however, would not budge easily. Bhabha's replacement, Dr. Vikram Sarabhai, travelled to Ottawa in late October to conclude the RAPP discussions with the DEA and officials from AECL. The Indians wanted the same conditions for both reactors, and objected on both technical and political grounds to Martin and Pearson's push for accepting IAEA safeguards on both technical and political grounds. The USSEA, Marcel Cadieux, attended the meeting and pushed the Canadian position that "agreement must be reached for the application of full IAEA safeguards to the Rajasthan station before the Canadian government could approve the financing of RAPP II." He was willing to compromise, provided the Indians reciprocated, "since it was evident quite early in the discussion that there would be no hope of progress without some accommodation on both sides." An agreement in principle was obtained. The solution was to treat the RAPP II reactor agreement as similar to the RAPP I agreement. Essentially, the IAEA would be asked to apply safeguards to both stations no later than one year after a reactor in each station became critical, but there would be no safeguards on future Indian-produced fissionable materials. Cadieux believed that the meetings had led to "a rather extensive paper which incorporates the essential provisions of the IAEA safeguards."[23]

Cadieux conceded that "it is regrettable that the Indians will not agree to have safeguards apply to later generations of fissionable material." But if the Indians accept this arrangement:

---

[22] LAC, RG 25 Vol. 10098, File 20-1-2 India pt. 2, Pearson to Indira Gandhi, August 2, 1966.

[23] LAC, Martin Papers, MG 32 B 12 Vol. 225, File 225-4 Commonwealth 1965–67, Memorandum from Marcel Cadieux to Paul Martin, November 4, 1966.

We will have resolved a critical issue in relations between Canada and India, made most significant progress in terms of Canada's policy on international safeguards and associated India with this policy to which they have been adamantly opposed since the early days of atomic energy. The benefits in terms of our bilateral relations with India and our international posture on such issues as the IAEA safeguards system and non-proliferation need no elaboration. It should also help us significantly with Pakistan. In view of the significant progress represented by the outcome of the negotiations with Dr. Sarabhai, and the most damaging consequences of a failure to reach agreement on RAPP II, I have no hesitation in recommending that you authorize us to continue technical discussions with the Indians on the attached draft with a view to reaching agreement on the basis outlined above. Do you agree?"[24]

Martin agreed with Cadieux's assessment. The proposed agreement was likely the best that could be secured unless Ottawa wanted to push New Delhi further, a choice that apparently had few takers.[25] On November 7, Basil Robinson wrote to Bud Drury, minister of industry and acting secretary of state for external affairs, to discuss the recent bilateral discussions. Robinson advised that "it is the judgement of Canadian officials, endorsed by Mr. Martin, that the proposed arrangements fulfil the condition for agreement established by Cabinet." The safeguards were essentially consistent with the IAEA system in all but one respect. This exception relates to safeguards on the second and subsequent generations of nuclear material originally produced in the reactor, a point covered in the IAEA Safeguards System but not in the 1963 Agreement. Indian officials are not prepared to extend the latter's provisions at this time to include this new element. Cabinet recognized and accepted the Indian position on this question when the 1963 agreement was concluded; it is the view of officials, which Mr. Martin has endorsed, that it would not be

---

[24] Ibid.

[25] It is worth wondering whether Ottawa had seriously thought of using its generous aid program as a "lever" to wring concessions. Although there has been reference to "levers," there was scant mention of using aid as a bargaining chip. Coincidentally, Indira Gandhi wrote Pearson directly in mid-November asking for additional food aid due to a drought that had ravaged the Indian countryside, affecting seventy million people. Gandhi asked directly for 500,000 tonnes of wheat to reach India by January. Pearson responded with a commitment to seek additional funds from Parliament "which would permit shipments of up to $21 million worth of foodstuffs from Canada over the next few months." There were strings however. Four million dollars would be used to purchase Canadian-produced flour. See LAC, Pearson Papers, MG 26 N4 Vol. 237, File 802/I39, Letter from Indira Gandhi to Pearson November 16, 1966 and Pearson to Gandhi, November 30, 1966.

desirable now to demand Indian acceptance of this additional principle as a condition of our agreement to finance RAPP II.[26]

On December 15, the RAPP II agreement received full cabinet support. Canada would contribute $38.5 million to the construction as well as technical support from AECL. Robert Winters, the trade and commerce minister, later hailed the agreement, stating "the sale confirmed Canada's position as one of the leading international suppliers of nuclear power stations."[27] The Canadian high commissioner, Roland Michener, was authorized to sign an exchange of letters setting forth the agreed principles and procedures on safeguards.[28] The Indian nuclear program therefore continued to benefit enormously from Canadian patronage.

The *Washington Post* applauded the safeguard concessions that the Canadians received from the Indians, suggesting that "India has taken an important new step toward abandoning its opposition to international inspection of its weapons-potential nuclear power plants."[29] The Indian press was not as delighted. The *Times of India* accused Ottawa of pressuring New Delhi, and Ottawa received a rap across the knuckles for evidently kowtowing to pressure from its Western allies and Pakistan in seeking such stringent safeguards. The *Indian Express* implied that New Delhi and Sarabhai had led India to being dependent on Western technology.[30] The Indian government downplayed the media scrutiny and released a statement asserting that India had not sacrificed anything to either the Canadians or to the IAEA.[31]

This domestic posturing, however, was only one piece of an increasingly complex international puzzle. The NPT negotiations in Geneva had become agonizingly slow and factionalized. The Indians wanted a level

---

[26] Ibid., Memorandum from Basil Robinson for Drury, November 7, 1966.

[27] LAC, RG 20 Vol. 1672, File 3-51-1 pt. 2, Department of Trade and Commerce News Release #24/67, February 28, 1967.

[28] The terms, particularly the foreign exchange portion of the project, were generous. The repayment terms provided a credit period of twenty years, including five years' grace on the repayment of the principal. The interest rate was 6% a year. At the same time, the United States, the IAEA, and India entered into a tripartite agreement for the supply of a small amount of US plutonium for Indian research purposes. See Perkovich, 131.

[29] See LAC, RG 20 Vol. 1672, File 3-51-1 pt. 2, the *Washington Post*, "India to Allow Check at A-Power Station," December 23, 1966.

[30] Ibid., Canadian High Commission to the USSEA, Despatch No. 68, January 31, 1967. See also, the *Times of India* "Sarabhai Defends Pacts With Canada," January 19, 1967; "Inspection," December 21, 1966; *Hindustan Times*, "No foreign inspection of a-reactors," January 19, 1967; The *Indian Express*, "Pact on atomic station 'not modified,'" January 19, 1967.

[31] Ibid., See Press Information Bureau of the Government of India "Expansion of Rajasthan Atomic Power Project," AEC Chairman' Statement, January 18, 1967.

playing field that ultimately prevented further acquisition of nuclear weapons by the current nuclear powers while preventing non-nuclear powers from developing a nuclear weapons capacity. This would have prevented China from threatening India by developing a nuclear arsenal while checking Pakistan's ability to develop a nuclear weapons capability. Additionally, New Delhi was open to guarantees from the nuclear powers that would meet its security concerns relating to nuclear attack or blackmail (Perkovich 2001). However, issues of disarmament, security guarantees, and discussion about the role of peaceful nuclear energy and even "peaceful nuclear explosions" were largely shunted to the background, much to the frustration of India.

By October 1967, it was evident that, barring major concessions from the nuclear powers, India would refuse to sign the treaty. Swaran Singh announced as much to the UN General Assembly, noting

> that while the Government of India continues to be in favour of the non-proliferation of nuclear weapons, it is equally strongly in favour of the proliferation of nuclear technology for peaceful purposes, as an essential means by which the developing countries can benefit from the best advances of science and technology in this field (Perkovich 2001).

Michener's replacement, James George, reported his concern at this hardening position to Ottawa. In turn, the DEA encouraged George to "make every possible effort to persuade the Indians to accede to the treaty" and to discuss it personally with Gandhi. The DEA sympathized that the NPT draft article on safeguards would discriminate against non-nuclear powers such as India, as it would apply effectively only to peaceful nuclear activities; however, on the issue of peaceful nuclear explosions, Ottawa firmly disagreed with the views of New Delhi. There could be no room in the treaty for this "since military and civil explosive technology are indistinguishable and development of a so-called peaceful nuclear device would accord non-nuclear states nuclear weapons." This clause, in particular, developed into the central sticking point between Ottawa and New Delhi. Ottawa believed that the NPT draft represented a series of gradual compromises and believed that it would be improved over the years. In the final analysis, the NPT "enhanced security for all non-nuclear states," which stood to benefit the most.[32]

---

[32] LAC, RG 25 Vol.10098, File 20-1-2-India pt. 2, R.D. Jackson to George, Despatch No. N-265, November 17, 1967. This despatch was also distributed to AECL and the PCO.

Ottawa slowly began to ponder the ramifications if India refused to sign the treaty. R.D. Jackson of the Disarmament division of the DEA advised George that he should give Gandhi the impression that, while not acting on instructions, he believed that Ottawa was "prepared eventually to tell the Indians that their failure to sign [the] treaty would not be understood by the [Canadian] people and might force reconsideration of Canadian-Indian nuclear cooperation."[33] Martin would be advised to take this line officially to Cabinet. The threat had little actual punch; no punishment would be immediately forthcoming, as the DEA was not ready to bring the matter to Cabinet.

George's meeting with Gandhi had little impact on the Indian position. On December 11, Gandhi proclaimed to the Lok Sabha that India did "not deem it proper at this time to go in for atomic bombs." George reported this to the department, concluding that the comment "represents of course no departure from the government's position as outlined a number of times in Parliament." The office of the USSEA was not so sure. D.M. Cornett replied to George that "after checking our files, however, we have the impression that it might represent a subtle, but deliberate, departure." While the DEA knew that the governing Congress party was critical of the NPT and this view was shared by numerous Indian opposition parties, "nowhere in their earlier parliamentary statements can we find so clear a reservation about permanently closing the nuclear option."[34]

Ottawa wanted to know the American and British positions in the hope of acting in concert with them if London and Washington thought it might have an impact. There was little cohesive action, however, as London and Washington pursued their own NPT agendas. For the time being, the DEA was willing to "maintain the pressure over the next few months" but was not "sanguine" about the eventual results.[35]

Despite the lack of progress in influencing Indian attitudes, George continued to approach the NPT matter with zeal. The Indians had recently asked Ottawa for an additional loan of $6.5 million for the completion of the RAPP I reactor. Perhaps, thought George, "it might serve as a gentle reminder to the Indians of our keen interest in their final decision" if Ottawa hedged on its final decision regarding the loan. He

---

[33] Ibid.
[34] Ibid., Vol. 10098, File 20-1-2-India pt. 3.1, D.M. Cornett to George, Despatch No. N-22, January 2, 1968. (See also George to DEA, Despatch No. 996, December 12, 1967).
[35] Ibid., R.D. Jackson to London & Washington, Despatch N-311, December 20, 1967 (the despatch was also sent to Geneva/ Delhi/ Rawalpindi/ Tokyo/ NATO/ the UN/ Rio/ Mexico/ Stockholm/ Moscow/ Vienna).

recommended that the Canadian government should not directly link India's acceptance of the NPT to whether or not it would receive the funding. On the other hand, he also added that it was not necessarily in Canada's interests to fund the Indian program at present.[36] The Economic division of the DEA disagreed, countering that Ottawa had "legal and moral commitments to fulfill" in terms of completing the reactor agreements."[37] The Indians would jump on the fact that they had already agreed on safeguards for the RAPPs, arguably creating more harm than good. This effectively ruled out one of the few "levers" Ottawa might have utilized.

The Commonwealth division supported that view, arguing that the "dominant opinion in the Indian Government at present is not to become a nuclear power." Besides, what would Canada do in the event that India still refused to sign the treaty? Would Ottawa continue to deny India the money "with the consequence that India sends its business elsewhere"? It believed Ottawa had little choice but to give the money. India was presently not a nuclear power, and it was still, officially anyway, mulling the NPT. The optics of Canada giving the money to India once it had disavowed the treaty would be terrible.[38]

Instead, the Commonwealth division asserted that Ottawa should rethink its strategy. Linking the continuance of Canadian nuclear assistance to India's signing of the NPT was a non-starter, and George's lobbying in New Delhi had accomplished little. By now the Indians surely knew of Ottawa's views. The Commonwealth division suggested that Ottawa might have some success if it directly approached Moscow, London, and Washington to jointly persuade the Indians to "sign and to provide something other than military guarantees as a suitable inducement." Indeed, the Commonwealth division even mused that Ottawa might act as a bridge between Moscow and Washington by making the first move in approaching the Soviets. Any success would have the added benefit of enhancing international relations, provided these parties could co-operate.

---

[36] Ibid., George to DEA, Despatch 3110, December 22, 1967. The Pakistanis, in the meantime, had pointed out, and George agreed, that "there is an element of contradiction between the professed Indian desire to keep a nuclear weapons option open and their formal assurances embodied in the 1956 CIR agreement and in subsequent statements by Govt. leaders that the products of the CIR reactor will be used for peaceful purposes only. The fact is that as long as India is dependent on sources of plutonium which are either under a peaceful use restriction (CIR) or under safeguards (RAPP) India has no military option, unless it should decide to violate one or the other of these agreements." George to DEA, Despatch No. 2976, December 8, 1967.

[37] Ibid., R.V. Gorham to George, Despatch No. E-112, January 2, 1968.

[38] Ibid., Memorandum from Donald Munro to Ralph Collins, USSEA, January 3, 1968.

Even if this failed, and its chances of success were slim, "We could never be accused of having lacked the imagination and courage to try every conceivable method of getting India to sign the NPT."[39] This was certainly creative, just as idealistic, and it failed as the Soviets were unwilling to antagonize the Indians as Moscow sought to develop its own "special relationship" with India.

The Disarmament division soberly noted that "there can now be no doubt at any level of Indian Government where we stand and how seriously we view the question of Indian accession [to the NPT]." There was some trepidation that these repeated approaches over the past months now risked becoming "counter-productive in terms of Canada-India [relations] and the Indian attitude to the NPT."[40] George confirmed that Ottawa could do no more: "We believe that we have gone as far as we can reasonably go at present in our efforts to modify strongly negative Indian views on NPT."[41] But George met Mrs. Gandhi one final time on the matter, hoping to persuade her in light of the recent Indian objection on another NPT draft in March 1968. The meeting did not go well, and George informed the DEA that Mrs. Gandhi's position had hardened. The Indians, he reported, "saw no real advantage for India in signing. Gandhi did not believe in anybody's guarantees of India's security." She argued that the treaty merely consolidated the status quo, with both the US and the USSR left unscathed by the treaty's provisions; France and China would simply ignore the NPT altogether. Mrs. Gandhi also rebuked George. He was, she said, "the only head of mission to have made representations to India on this subject." George insisted that he was only comparing "notes with her in view of our long and intimate collaboration with India in the atomic field which I hoped could continue in the spirit of confidence that would exist" if both nations were partners in an international control system held together by the NPT. This tactic did not soften the Indian leader and George saw "that she was unmoved by our arguments."

Perhaps, George recommended, Ottawa should continue to urge London, Washington, and Moscow to make their views more officially known to New Delhi in light of recent intimations that the Indians disingenuously considered discussions with those respective missions in New Delhi as "informal exchanges of views." In one of his last formal decisions on the India file, Pearson signed the despatch, noting, "I think we should be

---

[39] Ibid.
[40] Ibid., R.D. Jackson to George, Despatch No. N-51, January 30, 1968.
[41] Ibid., Vol. 10098, File 20-1-2-India pt. 3.2, George to DEA, Despatch No. 382, February 7, 1968.

careful about bringing pressure to bear on this matter."[42] Really, the Canadian policy had been overtly "careful." At no time was Canada's massive aid program to India chosen as a stick with which to rap the Indians on the knuckles. Instead, the Canadians quietly and resolutely pursued diplomatic channels, trying to sway the Indians with what they saw as rational arguments. As irrational as India's NPT views may have seemed in Ottawa, for the Indians their security was paramount. And for many Indians, adhering to the NPT threatened to weaken, not bolster, the fragile Indian security psyche. Canadians could afford to be rational on the NPT and act on their principles. Geography and the American strategic umbrella protected Canada. Canadian nationalists and supporters of a treaty banning nuclear weapons for countries that did not yet possess them might have objected to this stark assessment, but it was and remains true. India was poor, alone on a subcontinent, and largely boxed in by enemies against whom it had fought two recent wars, and it had precious few natural allies. The Indian nuclear program was constructed in good part for prestige and ambition at a time when the nation had scarce financial resources. It now had ample reasons to ignore the NPT and to develop a nuclear infrastructure. On April 5, Gandhi affirmed in the Lok Sabha that India would not sign the NPT. If, she said, some countries cut aid as a result, it would be "the first real step towards self-sufficiency." India would be guided by "our enlightened self-interest and considerations."[43]

In the end, Canadian attempts to persuade the Indians to sign the NPT and to accept full IAEA safeguards fell flat and Ottawa resigned itself to a *fait accompli*. For nearly two years, every other aspect of the bilateral relationship had been shunted aside by this one topic. Now, both countries were entering uncharted waters as far as nuclear co-operation and bilateral ties were concerned. George's efforts had little success and even within the DEA, the Commonwealth, Economic, and Disarmament divisions differed on what tactics Ottawa could adopt. Martin and Pearson had offered little top-down direction on both the safeguards and later, the NPT file—the brief and failed attempts at quiet diplomacy notwithstanding. One cannot help but wonder if both figures were simply swept along by the tide of events, such as the myriad domestic ills that plagued Pearson's minority governments, and whether the intricacies of a new Liberal leadership race, sparked by Pearson's decision in December to retire, acted as a final distraction during the final stages of the NPT

---

[42] Ibid, Vol. 10099, File 20-1-2-India pt. 4, George to DEA, Despatch No. 1186, April 5, 1968.

[43] Ibid., George to DEA, Despatch No. 1187, April 6, 1968.

negotiations. In April 1968, the new Trudeau government took the reigns of power and showed little interest on the NPT file or India for that matter, until the May 1974 peaceful nuclear device was tested in the Thar desert.

Canada-India Nuclear Negotiations: Context and Process

Ashok Kapur

Canada and India have a complex history of nuclear negotiations, nuclear co-operation, and a nasty spat. This history is the baggage, and Ottawa must decide whether to move forward with a new nuclear relationship or to stay the course with old attitudes and policies that have weighed it down since 1976 since. The history is important because it provides the context in which the nuclear question continues to be framed in Canadian governmental deliberations, particularly in the Department of Foreign Affairs in Ottawa.

The 1950s

There was a strong consensus between Canadian and Indian ministers, diplomatic mandarins, and atomic energy officials about the value of a special nuclear and diplomatic relationship, and its place in Canadian and Indian bilateral and international priorities and values. First, the nuclear question had an important diplomatic/international context: the practitioners sought to build Canada and India as two medium powers that had a motive as well as an ability to moderate the harsh aspects in the policies of the two superpowers. India's political and bureaucratic players found Ottawa receptive to their views of the Cold War (as Nehru did not in Washington), and Ottawa saw India as an influential player and a moderating influence to check Third-World radicalism with a voice in three international capitals—Moscow, Beijing and Washington. Second, Canada-India nuclear ties were stimulated by Eisenhower's "atoms for peace" proposals. They stressed the value of atomic energy co-operation and the place of atomic energy in national development and international co-operation. The Eisenhower proposal was an excellent cover and stimulus to build India's atomic energy community and to shape India's push for nuclear co-operation with Western partners, especially Canada, the UK, France, and the US. Finally, Canada's CANDU community saw a benefit in developing India as a showcase for its plutonium-heavy water-based technology in competition with the US-made light water-enriched uranium technology. In other words, all the Canadian and Indian ducks were lined up nicely to provide a strong critical mass of a political and a bureaucratic consensus at all levels: political-ministerial, diplomatic-bureaucratic, and atomic energy constituents.

In the early to mid-1950s, the international system did not possess a strong sense about the central role of international safeguards; the IAEA was beginning to take shape, but safeguards in the Canada-India context in the 1950s meant bilateral safeguards given India's suspicion of international inspections. Pushing the envelope from bilateral to international safeguards remained a contentious issue in Canada-India negotiations; India's grudging acceptance of weak, non-full-scope, international safeguards in the 1960s and 1970s was always a tradeoff to ensure reliable Canadian supplies. In the 1940s and the 1950s the Baruch Plan had failed to gain international acceptance, and the internal US debate about strategies to control atomic energy and the potential diversion to military uses remained unsettled in Washington. There was a proliferation of influential voices in America about ways to handle the nuclear question, and the "consensus" at the time was in favour of developing atomic energy co-operation and building the safeguards mechanisms, using atomic energy to build leverage bilaterally. Moreover, Canadians and Americans were content to accept Indian professions of peaceful intent at face value. Since 1948 Nehru and his senior atomic energy officials had stressed, in a public debate, the importance of peaceful uses and "other uses if compelled." The latter point was deemed to be hypothetical, and no effort was made by Ottawa to clarify the "other uses" or to take a firm position against it in the 1950s. The issue did not exist on the political radar in Ottawa at the time.

The 1960s

The Canada-India nuclear consensus weakened in the 1960s and, even though bilateral agreements continued to work and the negotiating process was robust with intra-Canadian and intergovernmental (Canada-India) controversies, the underpinnings of the consensus formed in the mid-1950s started to change. The balance of power among participants in nuclear questions shifted in the 1960s with the negotiation of the NPT; non-proliferation beyond the P-5 became the new norm, and international safeguards emerged as a benchmark to validate compliance with non-proliferation arrangements. As well, the number of bureaucratic players in Ottawa with competing agendas grew. Bilateral safeguards were the basis of the 1956 Canada-India agreement but with the acceptance of multilateralism as the basis of non-proliferation, tension emerged between bilateralism and multilateralism; that is, the underpinnings of Canada-India nuclear relations began to change in the 1960s. The bilateral negotiating framework rested on a balance between nuclear supply and weak bilateral-international safeguards and the importance of political relations and trust. However, in international conference diplomacy where Canadians were active, the balance shifted toward hard international safeguards and non-proliferation. Even before the entry into force of the NPT, Canadian and Indian practitioners had a contentious exchange about the meaning of "peaceful uses only"; this important aspect remained mired in secret controversy among practitioners in the 1960s. But with the NPT's entry into force, India's refusal to accept the treaty despite heavy Russian and Canadian pressure intensified the internal debate in Ottawa about India as an NPT holdout and the consequent implications for the bilateral arrangements. This was revealed in the Trudeau-Gandhi correspondence before the 1974 Indian test. The correspondence did not settle the issue because Trudeau emphasized Ottawa's problem with India's "peaceful" nuclear testing in the future and Mrs. Gandhi reminded Trudeau about the importance of bilateral obligations.

The 1970s

The 1974 test was the defining moment in the shift in Canada's nuclear and political relationship with India. Ottawa argued that the Indian action was a betrayal and contrary to the bilateral agreement. However, Canadian archives tell a different story. No agreement had been violated because the "peaceful uses only" clause was ambiguous, the NPT had a provision about PNEs, and there was a history of extensive but inconclusive diplomatic exchanges between Indian and Canadian practitioners about the interpretation of peaceful uses. In bilateral discourse the question was never settled. India's frame of reference, outlined by Nehru in 1948, was that India preferred to use atomic energy for peaceful purposes but it had the option to use it for "other purposes" if compelled. In 1948 and the early 1950s, the issue of Indian military applications was hypothetical. In the absence of an active Indian nuclear weapons program or a declaration of intent by India's political leaders about a nuclear bomb (Homi Bhabha, Nehru's chief atomic scientist, however, was open about his desire to build capacity for an Indian bomb), Ottawa's mandarins did not see a need to force the issue. Despite the fact that a) Bhabha had started advocating an Indian bomb and had alluded to India's nuclear weapons potential, b) the structure of India's nuclear program indicated a weapons potential, and c) US experts had concerns about Indian military intent, Ottawa ignored the subject because bilateral relations, "trust," atomic energy co-operation, and agreed safeguards trumped the nuclear question and international control of atomic energy. As well, the Canadian method was to observe Nehru's speeches carefully, and view positively his personal preference against the bomb and his well-known advocacy of global nuclear disarmament rather than assess the implications of the pattern of developments in Indian atomic science under Nehru's watch. As long as Nehru, an advocate of disarmament, and Krishna Menon, a convinced disarmer at all costs who influenced Nehru, held decision-making positions, Ottawa maintained a laid-back attitude because it felt that Nehru was keeping Bhabha and the bomb advocates in check.

The 1974 test shattered the political and psychological basis of the Canada-India nuclear relationship. This signal event created a strain; the tension between Canada's bilateral and its international (because of the NPT) obligations could not be managed quietly and a policy adjustment was required. Canada and India sought a negotiated solution during 1974–76. A draft agreement was initialed by both sides but the Canadian cabinet declined to approve it, and the effort failed with the termination of nuclear ties. Bilateral relations also went into cold storage. I have outlined the story of these negotiations in an article titled "The Canada-India Nuclear Negotiations: Some Hypotheses and Lessons" (The World Today, Chatham House, August 1978). I believe this article provides useful background to the 1974–76 Canada-India nuclear file.

Between 1976 and the time of this writing, the relations in the diplomatic, nuclear, and the economic sphere have maintained a cold-war stance—benign in the sense that the two are not killing or threatening each other as the Americans/Russians did, and because mutual indifference is better than public hostility; indifference and secret enmity can co-exist. But still there is a poisonous undercurrent in Canadian thinking that revolves around the theme of Indian betrayal and breach of agreement in 1974. This myth cannot be sustained by official records of the Department of Foreign Affairs of the 1950s and the 1960s; i.e., prior to the 1974 Indian test. The 1998 Indian tests reinforced Canada's non-proliferation concerns about India: in the blame game India was the provocateur, and Pakistan the respondent because India was the bigger threat to the smaller Pakistani minority and Pakistan had to defend itself—this was roughly the Ottawa logic.

Unlike Washington after 1998, Ottawa remains fixated with the Indo-Pakistani frame of reference and it has not recognized the triangular or multiangular basis of India's nuclear actions. Triangular because of the China-Pakistan versus India interface in the military and nuclear sphere; multiangular because NPT and CTBT diplomacy in the late 1990s (along with persistent regional strategic triangularity) sought to close India's nuclear option and increased the pressure on India to do something to escape international isolation. Ottawa's fixation with Indian nuclear weapons and the NPT, and a tender attitude toward the military government in Pakistan produced strange actions. When A. Q. Khan's activities were revealed along with signs of North Korean-Chinese-Pakistan nuclear and missile trade and transfer of Chinese nuclear test data to Pakistan—an obvious breach of NPT provisions—Ottawa said nothing, but when India conducted a missile test as part of a series, Foreign Minister Bill Graham expressed "regret." The lack of consistency on the nuclear and missile questions diminished Ottawa's credibility among Indian practitioners.

Lessons of Canada-India Nuclear History

This case history carries several key lessons. Governmental practitioners believe what they want to believe, and do not follow the evidence. Indian Prime Minister Indira Gandhi might have been faulted for not preparing the diplomatic groundwork for the 1974 nuclear test when she had capable Indian diplomats to do the work, but this is a criticism only of her inept style and the evidence in Canadian diplomatic records does not justify the sense of betrayal that is often voiced as the issue in Canada-India bilateral relations. The record indicates that bilateral agreements were not breached; furthermore, as early as 1948, Nehru outlined in a public forum the framework of India's nuclear policy: a preference for peaceful uses and an option for "other uses if compelled." Although "peaceful uses only" was highlighted in Canada-India agreements, as the bilateral controversy indicated, there was no agreed conclusion about the meaning of these words and there were extensive discussions about this issue among Canadian and Indian practitioners in the 1960s.

Negotiations in the context of intergovernmental controversies are affected by internal politics and domestic power politics. Intergovernmental negotiations go well if the ministers, diplomats, and scientists—the stakeholders in this case, are in tune with one another. This was the case in the early to mid-1950s in Canada-India relations. But by the 1960s and the 1970s the basket of issues and the cast of official players widened and became complicated. This was significant in the Canadian case: the new mix of players included nuclear suppliers and scientists (who favoured atomic co-operation under safeguards), India hands (who favoured bilateral co-operation), and on the other hand the anti-nuclear proliferators (who favoured multilateralism as the basis of a universal NPT regime). As a result of the development of the NPT regime and Canadian non-proliferation policy, the internal balance of power shifted toward the anti-proliferators and away from the bilateralists. This asymmetry has been maintained in Canadian policy since 1974. Absent a process of readjustment, Canada is stuck in its present mode of policy paralysis.

Going Forward by Learning from Past Mistakes

In such a situation, going forward is the alternative to a sustained policy paralysis and inaction. This is the first significant option that faces Ottawa's current political leadership; in this case, it requires an override of bureaucratic inertia that has produced the policy paralysis and a time warp in Canadian thinking about India and the nuclear question as it relates to India since 1974–76. Ottawa has not generated a single important, constructive, negotiable idea on the Canada-India nuclear question since the mid-1970s. This is a sad reflection on a country that sees itself as a knowledge-based society. "Going forward," on the other hand, is based on recognition that our knowledge about our friends and enemies is always imperfect. At the same time, however, changes in the external sphere create opportunities to grow, learn, and adapt through self-criticism and an acquired curiosity about our enemies—to understand their calculations and compulsions, their risks and opportunities, and thus frame new negotiating opportunities. Otherwise, imperfect knowledge and unwillingness to learn and adapt to external change produces policy paralysis and institutionalized rigidity that acquires a theological tone. This has been Canada's problem regarding the India question.

Allow me to summarize Canadian attitudinal mistakes that have become received wisdom in Ottawa and have skewed Canada-India nuclear policy and given it an institutional life.

a) India broke its agreements with Canada and is not to be trusted. This is a falsehood because India typically takes its international obligations seriously, and it has a good track record of fulfilling its nuclear commitments. It is true, however, that Indians are difficult negotiators.

b) The NPT is the foundation of international security and it works. This is a dangerous and an unnatural idea because the treaty was based on the anti-historical notion that arms races can be frozen by common cause among the major powers. The NPT produced the common cause among the P-5. China's conduct showed that it was more a believer in the Western school of power politics, and it accepted a privileged position for itself as a P-5 NWS. Then, having railed against superpower hegemony, it had no problem buying into a discriminatory international system as long as it received political compensation from fellow Great Powers. China's entry into the NPT system showed its acceptance of the common cause among the great powers of our time. But unless the arms race(s) in regions of conflict could be frozen, the NPT's foundation was shaky.

Whether or not the new entrants to the nuclear club acted on grounds that the international non-proliferation regime and its external rivalries threatened the new entrants' problem of survival and security and/or ambition and prestige, the Great Powers' common cause could not close the proliferation door. Securing rollback of nuclear programs in Brazil, Argentina, South Africa, and Libya is excellent window dressing because it obscures the reality of nuclear proliferation in regions of conflict where regional and international power rivalries abound—as in the cases of Iran-US, and India-China—and power asymmetries are sought to be addressed by countries located in regions of conflict. In this case the NPT system cannot, and is not, meant to problem solve regional-international geopolitical rivalries that involve the P-5 powers. The NPT policemen are also parties to geopolitical conflicts. Finally, it is not in their national interest to disarm and weaken themselves, choosing instead the window dressing that destruction of obsolete nuclear weapons constitutes progress towards disarmament.

c) Multilateral arms control trumps foreign policy and geo-politics and the NPT is a step to strengthen international society. Such a claim is bizarre because the bottom line in the definition of international society is that it rests on formation of common standards that apply to all. The NPT has one set of standards for NWS, and another for NNWS, and the distinction is maintained on the basis of a voluntary acceptance of non-nuclear status. This is a choice of a sovereign country and cannot be imposed by the so-called "world community." In the twenty-first century, many powers in the world have learned to adapt themselves to the notion that foreign policy and geopolitics trumps arms control, the opposite of the belief of die-hard NPT advocates.

d) Canadian relearning and adaptation is severely retarded because its frame of reference is tied to beliefs that India broke its nuclear agreement with Canada, that the NPT is a—or the—pillar of international security, and that multilateral arms control ought to trump narrow foreign policy and strategic interests in favour of views of the "world community."

Why Canada Should Learn from Its Past Mistakes, Stay in the Non-Proliferation Game and Build Its Diplomatic and Commercial Ties with India

These suggestions are based on a) an assessment of a dynamic process of international change that has altered the global and regional context of the nuclear question, and b) a major shift in the US approach that has thrown up a new rule set. The high point of the NPT—its indefinite extension and the CTBT resolution in the General Assembly—was also the beginning of the end of multilateralism as the basis of non-proliferation. Indian and Pakistani nuclear tests and declarations about their weapons status in 1998 undermined the diplomatic theory that the NPT was a pillar—if not the pillar—of international security. These mantras were deeply and widely believed by Canadian practitioners and some think tanks. But Ottawa is in a time warp because although Indian tests produced widespread international condemnation, this was followed by acceptance of India's nuclear weapon status as irreversible by the P-5 countries; on this basis, the major powers sought to bring India into the global mainstream by forming bilateral strategic dialogues with the new challenger of the NPT-driven world nuclear order. The US-India nuclear agreement (2005) and other signs of strategic partnership with India brought it into the global mainstream; India, in turn, was happy to join the world as an economic, diplomatic, and nuclear player.

The new agreements rested on P-5 recognition of India's positive role in changing Asian geopolitics and as a fit partner in promoting nuclear non-dissemination. But Canadian foreign affairs leaders under the Liberals (former Prime Ministers Jean Chretien and Paul Martin and former Foreign Minister Lloyd Axworthy) and the Conservative leaders under Prime Minister Stephen Harper are challenged in a number of ways. Canadian diplomatic theory and policy declarations do not acknowledge the importance of Asian geopolitics and the continent's growing importance as the centre of gravity of current international conflict (terrorism and nuclear and missile proliferation). Nor do they acknowledge the importance of building a post-NPT system of states that requires new bargains with the drivers in the nuclear scene. The problems of nuclear India, Pakistan, Iran, and North Korea are being dealt with by a small group of interested and effective players—the EU vis-à-vis Iran, Six Party talks vis-à-vis North Korea, and US-P-5-NSG vis-à-vis India. The new rule set and the set of players recognizes as well that the strains in the NPT come from among its members, and it is simply not enough to sign agreements without monitoring them and enforcing them effectively and in timely manner. These elements are necessary to give a rules-based regime a robust and credible character.

A new rules set is being developed by the US and its allies wherein they seek to form a new region-based nuclear order using the NPT as a reference point and a useful cover, but not as the driving element. Creating assured mutual dependencies between proliferating countries and major powers is the new driver; it is region- and context-specific, and the approach is not cast in abstract legal and moralistic terms. The aim is to create a web of new commercial and strategic links of which nuclear supply relations are a part, as is nuclear restraint. This way, the emphasis shifts to the development of incentives that are mutually beneficial to the stakeholders. The new approach relies on practical arrangements rather than moralism and legalism.

If we compare world relationships of the 1960s with developments since the 1990s, we can see that Ottawa's practitioners have been slow and inept in recognizing the implications of the changing approach to the nuclear question, as well as in acknowledging the changing redistribution of power in the world scene. Following international condemnation of the Indian tests, the NPT states differed in addressing the issues. Former Foreign Affairs Minister Lloyd Axworthy and his successors, as well as the Chinese government, remained opposed to moves to engage India. The Clinton administration, however, fenced off the nuclear question from the bilateral relationship and sought to broaden and deepen the latter; Canada, a self-styled middling power, remained indifferent. Axworthy and company maintained an anti-India position while China, Canada's co-advocate of Indian nuclear disarmament, practiced a double game of arming Pakistan with nuclear test data, technical aid, and a supply of North Korean and Chinese missiles and parts; at the same time condemning India for its China- and Pakistan-related actions. The line between principle and hypocrisy is thin indeed!

President Bush, the executive branch, and the US Congress changed the parameters of the US-India relationship. Going beyond President Clinton's approach—Clinton had moved US-India links from a cold-storage position on the nuclear issue to a thaw—Bush emphasized Indian democracy, its growing economic value, its role as a stabilizing force in Asia and a strategic partner, and its position as a non-proliferator. This was in contrast with Pakistan which, in the words of Senator Joseph Biden (quoted in *India Abroad*, December 1st, 2006, p. 13) did "more damage to the world than any single country [without starting a] war." This was a sea change; in the 1970s, Nixon-Kissinger-Chou-en-Lai had previously placed India in the category of a sub-regional country, on par with Pakistan. India now appealed to Washington in terms of political values, economic and strategic interests, and people-to-people contacts, including the support of Indo-Americans in American electoral politics. Between the 1960s and the 1990s, many Indian intellectuals and officials had expressed their resentment of Western indifference to Indian strategic concerns about Chinese nuclear weapons and Sino-Pakistani nuclear and military links and their negative effect on Indian security. The Indian intellectuals thought that the fixation with the NPT was overdone, and they thought little of the Western belief that the US-Russian condominium housing in the NPT negotiations was a source of international security. Finally, they were concerned with the problem of nuclear dissemination, a fear borne out by Chinese nuclear and missile dissemination to Pakistan and Pakistani dissemination and nuclear-related trade with Iran, Libya, and North Korea. (This trade involved Dr. A. Q. Khan and the use of Pakistani military aircraft to ferry banned nuclear and missile supplies to Pakistan from North Korea with Chinese facilitation and direct aid.) These widespread Indian concerns gained attention in Washington's psyche and policy establishment after 1998 and became a basis of US policy development. The result is well known. The Bush administration promoted an India-specific change in US non-proliferation laws, yet it did not offer a similar deal to Pakistan because of the difference in the non-proliferation behaviour of the two countries and the assessment of each country's importance to Western interests in the region and the world. The Bush administration was clearly creating a new road map in the world of global nuclear non-proliferation, Asian geopolitics, and South Asian international relations.

The US approach is innovative, a sign that despite its problems in Iraq it remains the only world leader that can think and act progressively in Asian strategic affairs and in international non-proliferation issues. Washington's method is to bring India into the non-proliferation tent by going around the NPT. This is necessary because of India's opposition to the NPT; the treaty's record to stop or slow proliferation where it matters the most (i.e., in regions of dangerous conflicts) is now worse than irrelevant. Its strains are the result of actions of the NPT members—Iraq, Iran, North Korea, and China. These countries broke the treaty rules by engaging in illicit nuclear exchanges. The treaty lacks an enforcement mechanism. Its disarmament provision is meaningless. The treaty's main value is that it provides cover for nuclear trade—legal and illicit without meaningful accountability of actions by the P-5 powers, especially China, in the recent past. The treaty also provides cover to national disarmament and arms control organizations whose themes are to peddle the possibility of nuclear disarmament in the future (without a time frame) and then claim that destruction of obsolete weapons was in fact progress toward disarmament.

But precisely because the NPT itself is practically a charade in places where it is needed the most (and it is effective in places where the danger of nuclear proliferation does not exist), going around the NPT has merit. This view rests on the proposition that just as the test ban norm has value in international relations without an enforceable legal international agreement on the CTBT itself (the General Assembly resolution lacks legal force), the non-proliferation norm has value in modern international relations. By going around the treaty, by not insisting on treaty adherence as a precondition for nuclear supply relationships among India, the US, other nuclear suppliers, and NPT states, by building a basket of interrelated incentives to form peaceful nuclear supply ties and disincentives against proliferation actions that disturb the peace in the future, the US-India deal represents real progress. It presents the prospects of nuclear energy co-operation as good commercial and political business; it brings India into the non-proliferation tent by recognizing that Indian policies and domestic politics preclude NPT and CTBT acceptance; it makes unilateral Indian restraint regarding nuclear testing a part of the basket; and it maintains by default calculated ambiguity about the "minimum/credible deterrent" as a basis of the Indian nuclear weapons program in relation to those who would try to pressure India by their nuclear weapons policies and/or their non-proliferation policies. Although there is no capping of Indian fissile material production, there is an expectation that India will work toward international negotiations to that end.

The US-India nuclear agreement has leveled the playing field in the sphere of nuclear negotiations between a "nuclear have" and a "nuclear have not" (under the NPT), and it signals that there are no free lunches if the approach is to formulate a system of mutual assured dependency between an international and a regional power. The NPT was a bargain between two superpowers that was projected as the basis of international security. The US-India deal is a bargain between an asymmetrical pair of powers that choose to come together in a challenging international environment at the beginning of the twenty-first century.

Canadian practitioners have a choice: they can either stay in the time-warped mental world of the mid-1970s or join the global mainstream of the twenty-first century. As China has begun to take India seriously in the economic and strategic spheres, it is a timely reminder to Ottawa to rethink the Canada-India nuclear and political question and either move forward and get into the game, or to opt out of it altogether.

Ottawa must learn to think outside the box if it is to maintain its credibility as a player in high security international politics. It has already lost its place as an interlocutor regarding North Korean arms control issues. It has been ignored regarding the Iranian nuclear question, and unless it changes its policy course and its rule set of elite attitudes that dominate a closed Ottawa policy community, it will become irrelevant or marginal in the Indian case. Open societies ought to be concerned about the implication of closed minds among their leaders and practitioners.

Nuclear Co-operation with India: Strategy, Economics, Environment

Ravi Seethapathy

Asian geopolitics have undergone a dramatic shift in the last fifteen years as a result of the rise of China, India, and the ASEAN countries as economic powers on the world stage. India too has shifted its policies and priorities radically since the mid-nineties to enshrine itself in this new paradigm.

Policies and Growth Imperatives

A short list of India's policy priorities include (a) playing a lead role in Asian geopolitics, (b) maintaining domestic economic growth, (c) ensuring that its energy needs are met, (d) securing finance for infrastructure development, and (e) developing bilateral economic ties. Its growth imperatives of managing opportunities for its 25 percent youth and economic uplift of its 70 percent rural poor largely hinges on its ability to maintain multisector economic growth of 8 percent which in turn is leveraged on energy security.

India is the only emerging growing economy in Asia that has attempted to balance its fuel needs strategically. For example, all its electricity production is based in indigenous fuel while oil imports are reserved for the transportation sector. Thus, although India employs almost all forms of technology and indigenous fuel mix (both fossil and renewable) in its electricity sector, it is still largely coal based. This indigenous fuel mix concept is something that India would like to continue while growing its economy, but it will face serious challenges because its increased production will give rise to a dramatic increase in greenhouse gas emissions. *This is where nuclear power mix will play a pivotal role.*

Impact of Growth

Economic growth is cumulative and time-based. For example, even a much lower 5 percent growth over thirty years would see a fourfold rise in per capita income, which would demand increased goods and services (consumption) and enable increase in capital formation (asset building) in its economy. Hence, its primary energy supply would have to grow at 6 percent (if not more) to keep pace. This would mean that India's electrical generation would have to grow to 750,000 MW from its current base of

130,000 MW. A good part of this initial increase would be due to India's high energy intensity level (as compared with China). All this would mean that its air emissions would potentially rise from 4 percent of global emission today to 40 percent in thirty years. Imagine what an 8–10 percent growth rate would do in thirty years.

As per 2001 statistics, India is fifth in the world (behind US, China, Russia, and Japan) in its carbon emissions at 250 million MT. This is a 61 percent rise from 1990 levels. Its per capita emissions at 0.25 MT are a mere 25 percent of the world average and twenty-two times less than the per capita of the US. However, by 2020 India will likely be at 0.75 MT per capita and will havemoved up to the top quartile. A good part of this increase will be due to the poor focus of India managing its energy intensity. For example, from 1980 to 2001 China's energy intensity (0.75MtC/k$) fell by 67 percent while India's (at 0.5MtC/k$) remained essentially flat over these twenty years. Part of the reason lies in (a) India still being a service economy and entering the manufacturing sector much later than China (in 2003), and (b) India's rural population still employing old technology/tools/applications for its livelihood.

India's Fuel Share/Balance

India has many attributes to its fuel balance. It has 250-plus years of coal reserves, which is good, but the coal has one of the highest ash contents (at 40 percent). Further, all its reserves are in the eastern part of the country, constituting transport distances of over 1000 kilometres to other parts where generating stations are located. In other words, 40 percent of the transport fuel and the coal transport tonnage is a waste (lower heat rate, transport congestion/cost). When all these costs are added up, the marginal fuel cost for the nuclear option becomes favourable when generation is located far away from the coal pitheads.

India has only 25 percent of its oil needs met from its domestic productions; 75 percent is imported and this is largely reserved for its transportation sector. On the nuclear fuel front, India has very little uranium reserves but plenty of thorium reserves. It has some hydroelectric potential left and fast-deploying renewable energy. But such renewable energy requires larger sustainable footprints (solar, wind, biofuel), and this in the long run could compete with India's much-needed improvements in agriculture and food production technologies.

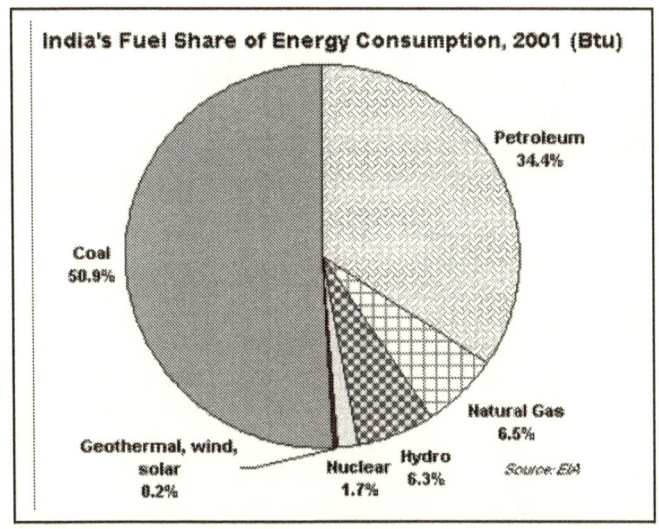

Figure 1: Energy consumption by source

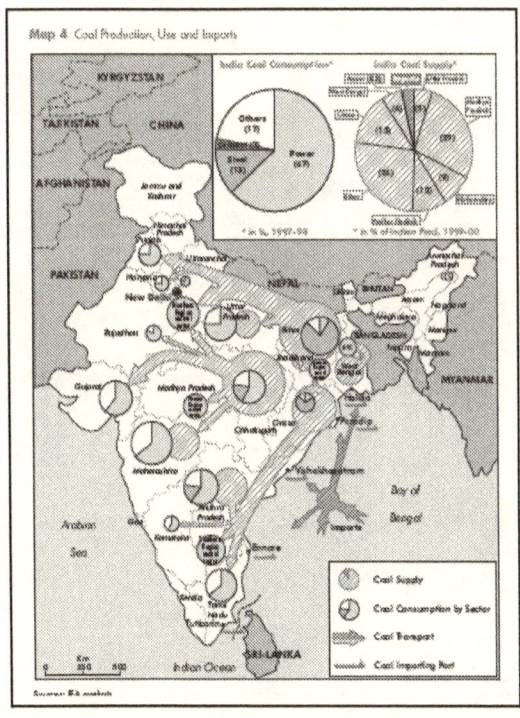

Figure 2: Coal production, use and imports

In effect, India produces its 128 GW electric power generation base with 90 percent of the fuel from indigenous supplies. It almost exclusively uses its oil (together with its 75 percent imports) for its transportation sector. This is quite an achievement for an emerging economy. In fact, this is a major aspect of India's maintaining its lower current account deficit.

India's Nuclear Fuel Challenge

India has about 54,000 MT of developed uranium reserves with a processing capacity of about 220 MT per year. Another 23,000 MT can be developed but is facing environmental assessment as well as local opposition. However, India's thirteen reactors alone need about 300 MT per year. This has resulted in its nuclear plants running at reduced plant capacity factors from 90 percent (2003) to 81 percent (2004) to 76 percent (2005). In other words, any more expansion of India's current nuclear technology fleet would result in more uranium imports to keep these plants running (hence the importance of the US-India agreement of 2005).

As explained in the earlier section, the locations of these nuclear power plants are far away from the eastern coal pitheads. Future nuclear plants will also be situated similarly.

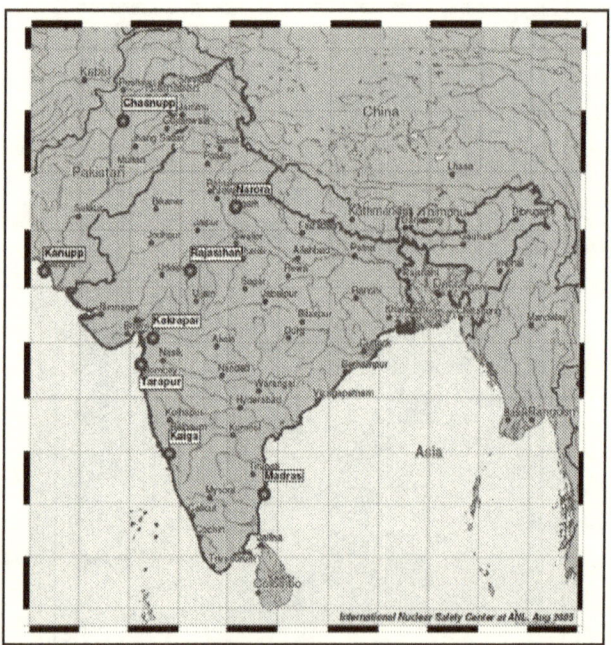

Figure 3: Locations of India's nuclear power plants

India has 25 percent of the world's thorium reserves at 290,000 MT. In order to leverage this fuel, India would need to embark on advanced reactor technologies (which it has). The fuel development for these advanced technologies would be in three distinct phases:

(i)   Produce plutonium through spent fuel reprocessing from its current uranium-fired reactors.

(ii)   Burn plutonium to breed uranium-233 from thorium blankets in fast breeder reactors.

(iii) Burn (33 percent) uranium-233 together with thorium (67 percent) to generate power in advanced reactors.

India's Electric Power Forecast

To achieve economic growth, India needs to triple its power generation from 128,000 MW to about 750,000 MW by 2030. But realistically speaking (given actual target shortfalls), it should be able to build about 480,000 MW. This would mean that a gap of about 250,000 MW would have to be managed through conservation measures as well as lowering of energy intensities (much like China).

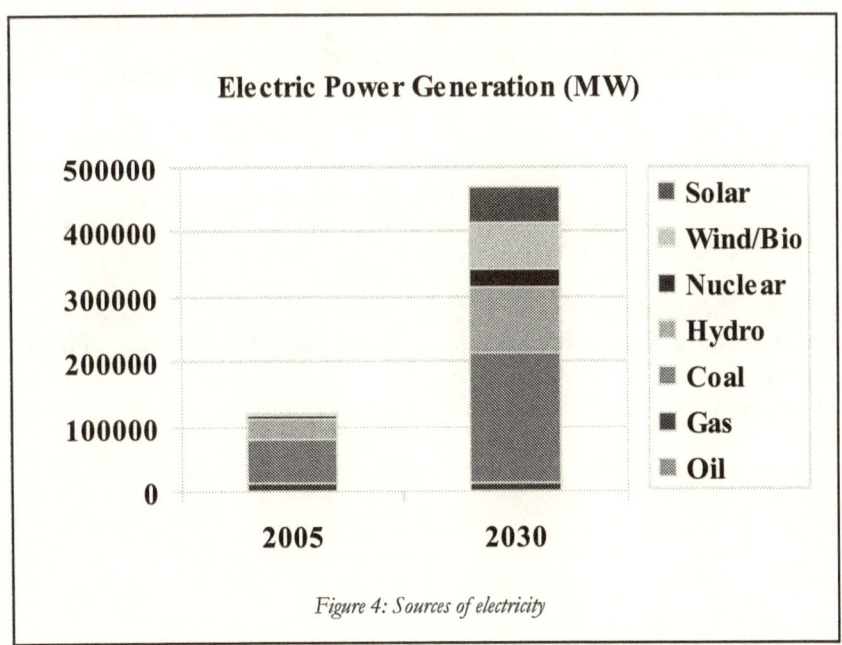

Figure 4: Sources of electricity

The impact of introducing even a small mix of nuclear in the energy portfolio is quite dramatic in terms of reducing future carbon emissions and coal intensity reductions. The nuclear mix is assumed at 10 GW (6.6 percent mix) and 30 GW (13.3 percent mix assuming the US-India nuclear agreement is fully implemented) by 2030. This is further augmented by implementing a pragmatic renewable energy policy.

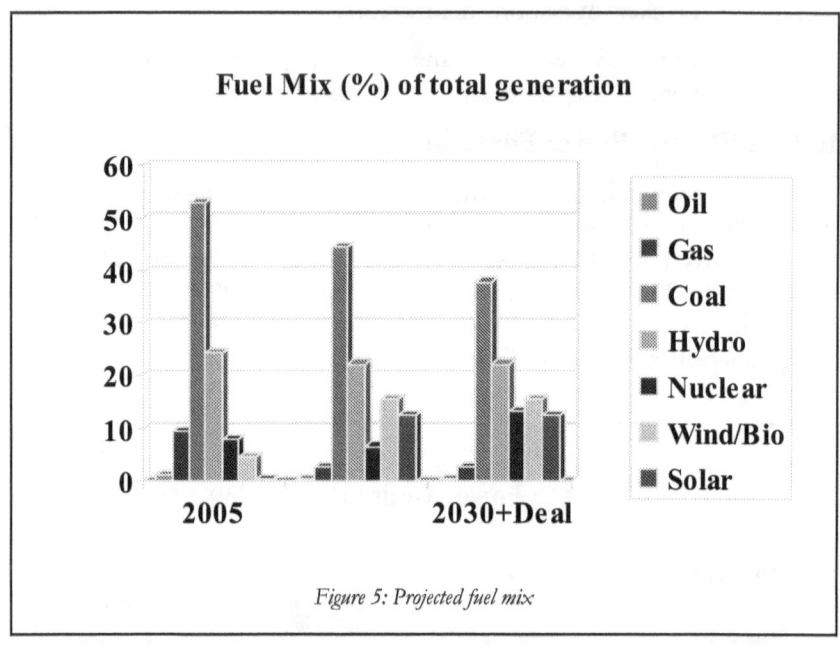

Figure 5: Projected fuel mix

In effect the overall reduction in CO_2 emissions is quite dramatic. The 17 percent reduction in emissions due to reduced coal-fired generation being taken up by nuclear (and renewable generation) is equivalent to 12 percent of UK emissions and 8 percent of emissions from the EU-25 countries.

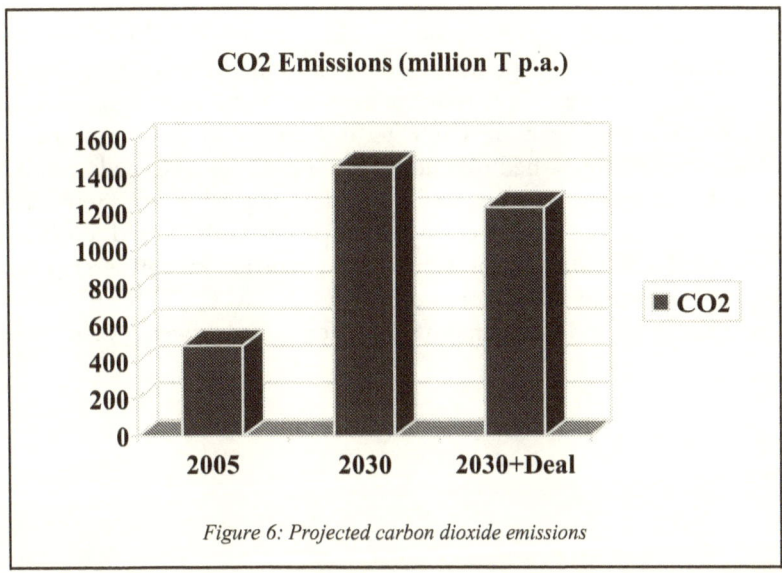

Figure 6: Projected carbon dioxide emissions

In fact, this is the same strategy being adopted by Canada for its Alberta oil sands to reduce CO_2 emissions in the future. By switching from gas to nuclear (to produce heat to extract oil from the oil-sands), Canada will reduce the 25 percent greenhouse gas emissions it currently produces from this project alone.

The US-India Nuclear Agreement and the Impact on NSG Countries

This agreement is important for both the countries since India gets to achieve its long-term nuclear technology thrust, reduction in coal transport congestion and emission reduction targets, while the US obtains a new relationship with India, specific nuclear inspections/safeguards as well as its private sector potentially participating in a $100 billion nuclear Engineering Procurement Construction (EPC) sector. Further, the US potentially addresses the China geopolitical factor going forward in its closer ties with India.

The impact of this deal within the NSG would also be beneficial to Germany, France, Russia, and Japan, which have many of the new (Fast Breeder and Advanced Reactor) technologies required by India. On the other hand, Canada will only benefit in the short haul based on its CANDU fleet and uranium supplies (both of which India needs in the short/medium term).

Thus, Canada needs to reflect on its India policy in light of the new paradigm and Asian geopolitics. Merely offering CANDU technology alone will not be an effective leverage as it was forty years ago. India has established self-sufficiency in CANDU technology in the meantime and has successfully refurbished two nuclear power stations. Canada needs to rethink its relationship with India for the long-term and rethink its position on the NPT as well. Such a policy shift would enable (i) extension of CANDU business in third countries in partnership with India, (ii) short-term supply of the 500/1000 MW CANDU reactors in the next ten years and (iii) uranium supply for the next twenty years or so.

The India-US Nuclear Deal: the Perspective of a Non-governmental Nuclear Scientist

R. Rajaraman

On July 18, 2005, Prime Minister Manmohan Singh and President George Bush announced a major agreement, including among other things a nuclear component, which took most observers by surprise. Although India had been seeking for some years the lifting of technology sanctions by the US, few people, barring those privy to developments behind the scenes at the highest levels, would have expected it to happen during that particular visit of the Indian prime minister—a visit that was largely ignored by the American media and considered something of a damp squib, until suddenly the agreement was announced.

The nuclear component of the agreement, commonly referred to as the India-US nuclear deal, was only one of many areas of co-operation listed in the July 2005 agreement. But it has become the most debated and controversial of all the items in the agreement. It has overshadowed the rest of the agreement and, despite two years of hard diplomacy since the original agreement, the different steps required for making the deal operational still remain to be completed.

Basically, the nuclear deal calls for India to identify and separate its nuclear facilities into civilian and military categories and place the former under international safeguards. In return the US would a) resume full civil nuclear energy co-operation with India, b) work with the US Congress to adjust US laws to enable such co-operation, and c) persuade the NSG to lift sanctions. This civil-military separation plan was negotiated between the two governments and announced in March 2006 in New Delhi. The details of the separation plan will be described in a later section.

The next step was to pass US legislation exempting India from sanctions and permitting the civil nuclear co-operation promised in the agreement. This was passed by the US House of Representatives in the summer of 2006, followed by the US Senate in November, and a joint version by both in December 2006. The resulting Henry J. Hyde Act was signed by President Bush into US law in mid-December 2006.

Getting the Hyde Act through the Congress amidst mid-term elections was an impressive effort of legislative management. But the Hyde Act is only an enabling legislation that lifts the sanction preventing the US government from entering into a nuclear agreement with India. The actual agreement that the two governments will sign, called the "123 Agreement," is still being finalized between them. Some contentious issues, especially involving reprocessing of spent fuel, persist at the time of writing. These will be discussed below. Once finalized, the 123 Agreement has then to be sent back to the US Congress for approval.

Parallel to these bilateral steps involving India and the US, other multilateral agreements also have to be concluded to make the deal fruitful. On one front, India-specific safeguarding arrangements of civil facilities have to be negotiated with IAEA. Consultations on this process have begun. Last but by no means least, the NSG, of which Canada is a member, must also agree to lift its sanctions. This step is far from being a formal endorsement and adoption of the US policy of resuming nuclear co-operation with India. As per their rules, the NSG decision has to be unanimous. Dissent by even one member can withhold nuclear co-operation with India. This, combined with the perception that many NSG member countries have serious non-proliferation concerns about the agreement makes the passage of exemption by NSG far from trivial.

This is a summary of the position today. Meanwhile, the past two years, consumed in setting up the nuclear deal, have seen intense debate in India and abroad and given rise to widely different perceptions on its implications. In this essay I will go back and analyze the implications of different aspects of the deal, but from a different perspective from what has been generally available, viz., that of an independent non-government scientist in India.

The Separation Plan

All nuclear facilities in India belong to one governmental department, the Department of Atomic Energy (DAE). There are no nuclear plants or materials in the private or academic sector, other than small amounts of radioactive material in research labs and hospitals. The DAE is a large and well-endowed organization with about fifty facilities, shown in the map below. These had to be separated into a civilian sector and a military unsafeguarded sector.

Atomic Energy Establishments in India

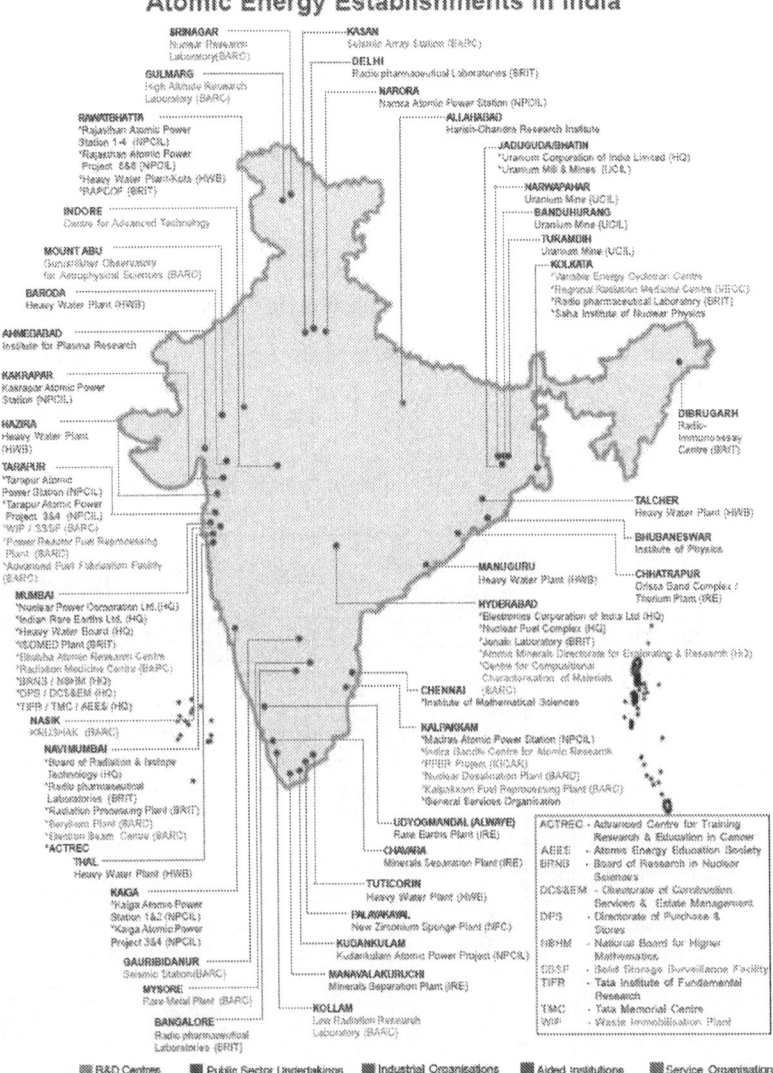

Figure 1: Atomic energy establishments in India

Of these facilities, some are minor and others are obviously either civil or military. The main items under contention with regard to separation were:

(i)   Fifteen operating power reactors, of which four are already under safeguards, and eleven reactors whose status had to be decided upon.

(ii)   Seven more power reactors under construction (two safeguarded).

(iii)   The Fast Breeder Reactors—the baby test reactor (40 MW) and the Prototype Fast Breeder Reactor (PFBR) under construction.

(iv)   The plutonium reprocessing plants.

(v)   All the spent fuel accumulated so far.

(vi)   The Rattehally uranium enrichment facility.

The separation of the fifteen power reactors in operation and seven under construction in India into civilian (to be open to safeguards) and military (to remain unsafeguarded) categories as agreed by the two countries in March 2006 is shown in Table 1. Altogether there are fourteen safeguarded (4380 MWe) and eight military (2350 MWe).

Power reactor	Type	Gross power (MWe)	Start-up date	Safeguards (June 2006)	Open for safeguards
In Operation					
Kaiga-1	PHWR	220	16-Nov-00	No	Military
Kaiga-2	PHWR	220	16-Mar-00	No	Military
Kakrapar-1	PHWR	220	6-May-93	No	2012
Kakrapar-2	PHWR	220	1-Sep-95	No	2012
Madras-1	PHWR	170	27-Jan-84	No	Military
Madras-2	PHWR	220	21-Mar-86	No	Military
Narora-1	PHWR	220	1-Jan-91	No	2014
Narora-2	PHWR	220	1-Jul-92	No	2014
Rajasthan-1	PHWR	100	16-Dec-73	Yes	Safeguards
Rajasthan-2	PHWR	200	1-Apr-81	Yes	Safeguards
Rajasthan-3	PHWR	220	1-Jun-00	No	2010
Rajasthan-4	PHWR	220	23-Dec-00	No	2010
Tarapur-1	BWR	160	28-Oct-69	Yes	Safeguards
Tarapur-2	BWR	160	28-Oct-69	Yes	Safeguards
Tarapur-4	PHWR	540	12-Sep-05	No	Military
Under Construction (Planned Dates)					
Kaiga-3	PHWR	220	2007	No	Military
Kaiga-4	PHWR	220	2007	No	Military
Kudankulam-1	VVER	1000	2007	Yes	Safeguards
Kudankulam-2	VVER	1000	2008	Yes	Safeguards
Rajasthan-5	PHWR	220	2007	No	2007
Rajasthan-6	PHWR	220	2008	No	2008
Tarapur-3	PHWR	540	2007	No	Military
PFBR	Fast Breeder	500	2010	No	Military

Table 1: Civil-Military Separation of India's Operating Reactors

In addition to the reactors, other facilities that were allowed to remain *unsafeguarded* were:

(i) The Dhruva (100 MWth) and Cirus (40 MWth) Pu production reactors.

(ii) The Fast Breeder Test Reactor (13 MWe).

(iii) The Prototype Fast Breeder Reactor (PFBR; 500 MWe).

(iv) Pu reprocessing plants:

    a. Trombay   50 HMt/y

    b. Kalpakkam   100 HMt/yr

    c. Tarapur   100 HMt/yr

(v) Uranium enrichment plant (~5000 SWU).

(vi) All the spent fuel stocks until safeguards are in place.

The Public Debate: An Important Side-Benefit

This separation plan was not easily arrived at. It took more than six months of negotiations and much public debate. The debate in India was unprecedented and, in my opinion, an important but not sufficiently acknowledged side benefit of the deal. Two major areas of activity in India had hitherto rarely been subject to any public discussion, either in the mainstream media or Parliament. One was the functioning, policies, and performance of the Department of Atomic Energy (DAE). The DAE had been protected from the hassle of public scrutiny and criticism, in part because of tradition—the prestige of Dr. Homi Bhabha, who founded it, and his close access to Prime Minister Nehru had given the DAE a special status—and in part because of its involvement with nuclear weapon development, which automatically endowed it with some secrecy on national security grounds.

The second area about which there had been little public discussion was the implication of India's stated policy of "minimal nuclear deterrent" in concrete terms, with respect to the size of its nuclear arsenal that was needed to set up such deterrence.

The process of arriving at a civil-military separation plan opened up both these "sacred cow" domains to public scrutiny and discussion. During the negotiations in the fall and winter of 2005, the Indian side (in particular the DAE) pressed for keeping as much of its nuclear activities outside safeguards as possible, while the US representatives in turn argued that unless a substantial fraction of Indian reactors came under safeguards, there was not much hope of the deal getting past the US Congress and the US non-proliferation lobby. The status of India's Prototype Fast Breeder Reactor under construction at Kalpakkam was the main bone of contention. As this tussle between the two sides continued, the DAE brass—its current and retired senior officials—went public with arguments for why the PFBR and a fleet of supporting CANDU-type reactors needed to be placed inside the military fence. First they claimed that placing the PFBR under IAEA safeguards would seriously hamper its research and development work (Subramanian 2005). Later they raised the ante by adding, ominously, that it would also jeopardize "national security" (Bagla 2006).

This was a somewhat surprising step. The DAE is an arm of the Indian government, and its chairman a technocrat whose status is that of a civil servant. Generally it is not the practice in India for civil servants to publicly air their own views or even the views of their departments, especially on such sensitive matters. Political leaders of the opposition parties do attempt to influence the government's position by voicing their opinions publicly and so do various experts and commentators not belonging to the government. But within the government, even individual members of the ruling cabinet are not expected to independently air their views. They are expected simply to follow the collective decision of the cabinet. And civil servants, although vested with arguably the largest role in the government's internal policy-making process, are generally not meant to discuss these policies in public, except when explaining policies already approved by their political leaders. For instance, India's commerce secretary would not publicly offer his own views on what India's negotiating position should be at the WTO. He would do that only in closed-door consultations with his colleagues and his ministers in the cabinet. Nor would the finance secretary comment on aspects of the national budget while it is under preparation. Given this tradition, it was quite unusual of DAE officials to have laid down major conditions on the Indian government's bargaining position on the Indo-US deal even while the negotiations were in early stages.

Were the DAE's public pronouncements, seemingly out of order, made at the behest of the government leadership to strengthen the latter's hand in making correspondingly tough demands on the Americans? Or were the DAE technocrats acting on their own, confident of their independent clout and their public image as scientists who had made the nation safe and proud by producing nuclear weapons? There was some speculation about both these possibilities, and the true answer is not publicly known even now. Regardless, an ironic consequence of the DAE going public with its strong conditions, partly to protect the agency's own autonomy and turf from outside intrusion and scrutiny, was that it had the opposite effect.

My collaborators and I had pointed out early in the game that the civil-military separation plan in effect called for a quantitative estimate of how large a nuclear arsenal India really needed (Rajaraman 2005b; Rajaraman 2005c). The policy goal of building a minimum deterrence capability had to be translated, first into the number of nuclear warheads required for that purpose and then into the amount of fissile material needed for making that many weapons. Only then could a rational decision be made regarding which facilities had necessarily to be placed inside the military fence to ensure that the required quantity of fissile materials could be produced. No rational estimate of this sort was available when the deal was first announced in 2005—at least not in the public realm.

Eventually this linkage between the separation plan and the nuclear arsenal was recognized and picked up by several commentators in mainstream think tanks and the media. When the DAE's conditions on the deal, amplified by the political Left, threatened to distinctly slow down—if not scuttle—the negotiations, those sections of the media and the strategic community that felt the deal was important and beneficial began examining the DAE's arguments in some depth. This generated greater awareness about fissile materials and the quantities produced by the different nuclear facilities. It also generated debate on the desired size of India's nuclear arsenal and the consequent fissile material requirements of India's strategic program. The civilian energy program, its past rate of growth, and future projections also came under debate, as well as the shortage of uranium for these purposes. It was very heartening for this author to see political scientists and members of the media striving to pick up the basic physics of uranium, plutonium, fast breeders, and so on, in order to make educated judgments on different facets of the deal.

Regardless of where the nuclear deal ends up, the partial opening up of India's civilian and military nuclear activities to public checks and balances is, in its own right, healthy for the country.

Is the Agreement Good for India?

It seems to me the agreement is very good from India's point of view. True, it has its imperfections from the Indian point of view—but no deal is ever perfect from either side's viewpoint and, after having negotiated hard, compromises have to be accepted by both sides. In the end the benefits of the deal have to be compared with not having the deal at all. If the nuclear deal (including the NSG endorsement) becomes fruitful, sanctions will finally be lifted. The long isolation of India's nuclear program will have ended. It can hope to build more reactors faster and enlarge its nuclear energy program to meet the surging demands for energy in the coming decades. A near 10 percent annual growth in GDP that India is hoping for in the coming years will necessarily be accompanied by a correspondingly heavy requirement for energy. To meet this demand, energy generating capacity using all forms of renewable and non-renewable sources will have to be greatly enhanced. On the nuclear front, about 3 GWe of energy is being generated at present, constituting only about 3 percent of the total electrical energy produced. Even completion of reactors currently under construction will increase this to only about 6 to 7 GWe, whereas the government has variously made projections of a generating capacity of about 30 GWe by 2020. Thus a much larger expansion is called for, and within a short time. This can only be done by concerted reactor building through collaboration with several countries. Without the US-India agreement, much of this would be impossible.

India's Uranium Requirements

Once the deal comes into being, India can also purchase badly needed supplies of uranium. The shortage of uranium for our nuclear energy plans is sometimes disputed. India's uranium ore is undeniably limited and not of the highest quality. How bad the shortage is depends of course on how much nuclear power needs to be generated.

India's uranium requirement for existing and under-construction reactors is about 675 metric tonnes. In contrast, current production of uranium is only about 300 tonnes a year (600,000 tonnes of ore of 0.05 percent uranium content). Efforts are underway to open new mines that may yield 150–200 tonnes more. That would still leave a shortage even for reactors currently operating or being constructed.

If India wants to produce up to 30,000 MWe capacity as the government would like it to do, it will need about 4,300 tonnes of uranium a year! Even if India could mine uranium that fast, it will run out of underground ore soon. According the authoritative "Redbook" on uranium resources (Anon 1998a), the known conventional *in situ* resources include 54,800 tU under the Reasonably Assured Resources (RAR) category and 29,800 tU under Inferred Resources (IR) categories. There may in addition be about 29,000 tonnes in the "undiscovered resources" category. This gives a range of available uranium from an assured 54,800 tonnes to an optimistic maximum of about 114,000 tonnes. That can fuel 30 GWe worth of reactors only for 13 to 27 years. Thus, India certainly does not have enough uranium ore for such large generating capacities for any significant length of time. This is a major motive behind the agreement that will enable India to import uranium.

Concerns in India about the Agreement

Despite these advantages to India, some groups began to express serious concerns about the agreement. As mentioned already, leading DAE officials, current and retired, repeatedly cautioned that the deal would a) handicap the development of its civilian energy program, creating intellectual property problems and procedural delays due to safeguarding, and b) compromise India's strategic program through fissile materials capping and restraints on future nuclear testing.

In addition, there were fears that the agreement brought with it constraints on India's hitherto independent foreign policy (like the Iran issue). The Indian Left, which had always had a generic allergy to entering into any deals with the US, gave political support to all these apprehensions. There were also more technical worries such as the right to reprocess the spent fuel, guarantees of fuel supply, and the right to build up a fuel reserve.

Some Indian apprehensions were addressed during 2006. In the six months that the US waiver legislation went from House and Senate discussions to the final Henry Hyde Act, many US demands that fuelled such concerns were diluted or dropped. Amendments by Senator Russ Feingold on the impact of the deal on India's weapons program, and by Senator Barbara Boxer requiring Indian action on Iran, were voted down. Section (106)(a)(1 and 2) of the Senate Bill S 3709 (dealing with exports of enrichment and reprocessing technology) has been softened in Section 104 (d) 4A(i) of the final Hyde Act. In the House bill, section 4(d) 2 and 3 calls for automatic termination of deal if some NSG guidelines are not met. This too is absent in the Senate bill and the final Henry Hyde Act.

Unresolved Issues

A few concerns still exist from the Indian side at the time of writing. The main amongst them are: a) the impact of the deal on India's conducting a nuclear test, b) whether India can reprocess the spent fuel of imported reactors and whether reprocessing technology can be transferred to India, and c) a guarantee of lifetime fuel supply for the imported reactors.

These are, in this writer's opinion, *comparatively* smaller matters when placed against what has been negotiated already and hopefully will not be allowed to derail the agreement at this late stage (Rajaraman 2007). Let me elaborate on this a little.

Testing

In substantive terms, the issue of "testing" is really the least serious of the items under negotiation at the present. Of course India's sovereign right to conduct nuclear tests is a serious matter. But the impact of the Indo-US agreement on this right is minimal in substantive terms. It should be stressed that the 123 agreement cannot "prevent" India from testing. It can only threaten to render the agreement on nuclear co-operation null and void, if India ends up testing. As a sovereign country, India can always conduct further tests if chooses to do so after carefully weighing its strategic requirements against its nuclear energy requirements. At the same time, however, it has been known all along that if India were to conduct another nuclear test, all nuclear co-operation would have to be suspended by the US. This is regardless of what is or is not mentioned in the 123 Agreement. The relevant portions of the US Atomic Energy Act demanding such sanctions exist separately from, and irrespective of, the Hyde Act passed in 2006.

The only point of contention is whether a clause to this effect should be explicitly mentioned in the bilateral 123 Agreement or not. India would prefer to leave its moratorium on testing as a unilateral one, rather than be bound by a bilateral treaty. This is largely a legal and diplomatic distinction, and it would unwise for either side to insist on having its way on this singular point at the cost of jeopardizing the entire deal.

Reprocessing

The issue of reprocessing spent fuel is a more serious matter, and the DAE's concerns in this regard are understandable. A situation where India can neither reprocess spent imported fuel nor give it back to the original suppliers is clearly undesirable. India's only recourse, then, would be to store radioactive spent fuel, as is happening in Tarapur.

But here too, we must focus only on the actual constraints that the Americans want to write into the 123 document and not extrapolate beyond them to fret over imaginary contingencies. Unfortunately, while news reports continue to mention reprocessing as the thorniest issue holding up the agreement, they also continue to be vague about some critical details on what exactly the US position is. If the US demands are only that a) it will not supply India with reprocessing technology, and b) it will not allow India to reprocess the fuels supplied by them for the reactors India buys from the US, then this is a problem we can live with, should worse come to worst. True, the Americans do exempt some other countries from these restrictions, and up to a point it made sense for India to keep pressing that it be treated on par with those countries. But beyond a point, it is not worth abandoning the deal for that reason alone.

Remember that if the deal is completed and accepted by the US Congress and the NSG, in all likelihood the first batch of reactors India buys will not be from the US but from Russia or Areva, the French nuclear giant. Both these nations are poised to enter into reactor trade with India and preliminary negotiations have already taken place. There are indications that the Russians may be willing to sell India both reactors and their fuel without such strings attached. In that case, the India-US deal, a bilateral treaty, cannot prevent India from building its own reprocessors, and reprocessing spent fuel from a third country, say, Russia. Alternatively, the Russians may agree to take back their spent fuel so that India is not stuck with it.

Of course, the NSG may pass its own strictures against India reprocessing any imported fuel. But if India agrees to reprocess under IAEA supervision and transparently shows that the reprocessed plutonium will be used only for civilian energy and not weapons, it would be churlish for the NSG to deny that.

Concerns Expressed Outside India

Indian concerns over elements of the deal have received a lot of exposure in the Indian media and intelligentsia since the entire agreement is considered an important issue there. But there have been a different set of concerns expressed *outside* India about the agreement, particularly by non-proliferation experts. These may be summarized as follows:

(i)   The agreement leaves India with considerable unsafeguarded capability for producing weapons-grade fissile material, should it choose to do so. The apprehension this has created is ironic, since critics in India are worried about the exact opposite, namely that the deal will hinder India's capacity to produce a sufficient number of warheads!

(ii)   India may be able to spend all its indigenous uranium ore for military purposes since the agreement allows it to import fuel for its civilian reactors.

(iii)   The deal may accelerate the arms race in South Asia.

(iv)   By giving special exemption to India, the deal may undermine the NPT regime and other non-proliferation efforts.

Let us examine some of these issues. For item (i) above, my colleagues and I did some calculations to see how well founded these fears were.

Among other things we calculated the quantity of weapons grade plutonium that India can produce in its unsafeguarded sector, if the deal goes through. Table 2 gives a quick summary of our findings.

Reactor	CIRUS (Until 2010)	Dhruva	Breeder (after 2010)	Spent already	Total stocks	Weapon equivalent
Cumulative production (kg) to date	234	414		-130	~ 520	104
Annual future production (kg)	9	20-25	135		~ 160	32

Table 2: Annual weapons-grade Pu produced from unsafeguarded reactors[1]

Although the US-India agreement will *permit* about 160 kg of weapons-grade plutonium (equivalent to about 32 weapons of the 20 KT category) to be produced annually, this should not be attributed to the deal. Even if there had been no deal and sanctions had continued, these three reactors—CIRUS (till 2010), Dhruva, and the PFBR—would be operative in the future and produce those 160 kg of Pu. Since everything would be unsafeguarded in the absence of the deal, India could continue to accrue that much weapons-usable Pu anyway. By the same count, Table 2 should also put to rest the argument, used by some Indian critics of the deal, that it would restrict India's strategic capability. The capability given in the table would remain, irrespective of the deal.

The estimates above were made on the assumption that the eight unsafeguarded water reactors placed inside the military fence as per the separation plan will not produce weapons-grade Pu. But if one or more of those reactors were to be run on "low burn," it could generate weapons-grade plutonium. That would require feeding in much more uranium fuel for a given power output than is normally required. Now, India's limited availability of indigenous uranium is not enough even for running the existing reactors in a normal mode and there would be no question of running one of its large power reactors in a significantly low burn mode. But item (ii) in the concerns listed above raises an alternate possibility. If the deal goes through and India is able to import all the uranium for its

---

[1] This and the following table are based on calculations by Z. Mian, A. H. Nayyar, R. Rajaraman, and M.V. Ramana. These calculations were conducted at a summer visit to Princeton University's Program on Science and Global Security.

civilian sector, that would free all its indigenous uranium for the military sector. Could this be used to run one of the eight unsafeguarded reactors at a low burn level and produce weapon grade Pu? We investigated this question in some detail.

Using Surplus Uranium to Make Additional Weapons-Grade Plutonium

First, let us estimate the amount of domestic uranium surplus available as a result of the deal that could be diverted for military purposes. Most of India's domestic uranium would of course be needed to fuel the eight heavy water reactors placed inside the military fence. In the next few years, the domestic uranium demand for India's unsafeguarded reactors will increase further by about 140 tonnes per year, to 575 tonnes per year, as the 540 MWe Tarapur-3 and the 220 MWe Kaiga-3 and Kaiga-4 reactors are completed and begin operation in 2007. However, the total domestic uranium requirement will begin to decrease as some of the currently unsafeguarded reactors are opened for inspection in 2010, 2012, and 2014. As well, as the Rajasthan 1 and 2 reactors can be fuelled with imported uranium (Table 3). As the table shows, the annual uranium requirement will fall to about 340 tonnes. To this one must add another 35 tonnes for sundries like the Dhruva reactor, making a total requirement of about 375 tonnes per year. If the planned additional uranium mines are fruitful and increase the production to about 450–500 tonnes annually, this would result in a surplus of about 75–125 tonnes.

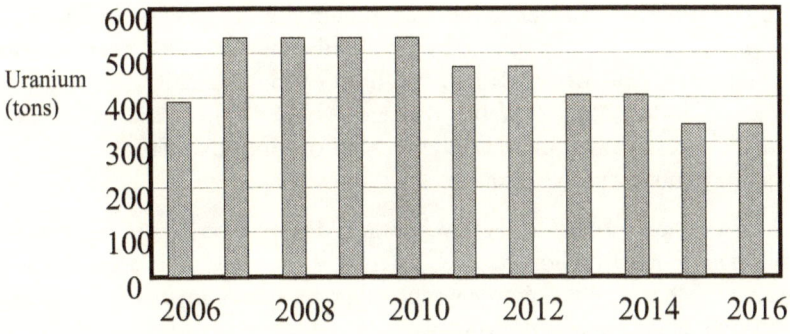

Table 3: Domestic uranium requirements for safeguarded reactors

One way to use this excess uranium for weapons purposes is for India to run one of the eight unsafeguarded 220 MWe PHWR at low burn-up, so that it would yield weapons-grade instead of reactor-grade plutonium. At a burn-up of 1000 MWd/t the reactor will consume 222 tonnes of uranium a year, i.e. about 190 tonnes more than the normal 7000 MWd/t burn-up. Hence, even a surplus of 75-120 tonnes can allow you to run only a part of the PHWR at low burn-up. But you can recycle the slightly depleted uranium (0.6 percent U-235) from this production reactor to partially replace natural uranium in the remaining seven PWHRs, saving about 20 percent, i.e. about 60 tonnes. This, along with the surplus of 120 tonnes can, in principle, run almost a full PHWR in production mode producing about 200 kg of weapons-grade plutonium a year, on top of the 160 kg a year from Dhruva and the breeder reactor.

But this is a very convoluted procedure. In practice the weapons-grade Pu output will be limited by how fast fuel can be reloaded for low burn-up, how fast the depleted uranium can be reprocessed, and how much uranium is available to be mined. The estimate of 200 kg/year should be viewed as the theoretical maximum of what can be produced with the surplus uranium. The actual output, even if this procedure is adopted, will be much less.

Is India Likely to Make So Many Weapons?

I do not believe India plans to use the India-US agreement to enhance its nuclear arsenal. India's nuclear doctrine (Anon 1998b) calls for "credible minimum deterrence" which, when examined objectively and without cold war preconceptions, does not require anywhere nearly as many weapons as the production capacity estimated in the preceding section permits. I have been arguing this for some time (Rajaraman 2005a).

Briefly, minimal deterrence neither requires a boundless open-ended arsenal, nor that the weapons match in number and strength those of your adversaries. It only demands that you have enough capability, in a second strike, to inflict "unacceptable damage" to the other side. The really difficult question to answer in any sort of objective fashion is what constitutes unacceptable damage.

A half-a dozen modest 20 KT weapons if dropped on major Asian cities could kill about a million people. Surely, that is more than enough to be unacceptable to even a remotely rational government anywhere, including Pakistan's and China's. All you need are a couple of dozen weapons in store that can provide sufficient redundancy and account for survivability, etc., and ensure such a modest second strike. Accuracy is not so important for counter-value strikes.

If the adversary is controlled by such irrational and suicidal leadership that they find a million immediate civilian deaths acceptable as a price for military adventure (as can conceivably happen) then one cannot logically guarantee that a much larger arsenal will deter them anyway. Any policy of deterrence has to assume, rightly or wrongly, that the adversary is rational.

I am not claiming that my estimate of just a dozen surviving deliverable weapons as sufficient for deterrence is shared by the Indian establishment. But even as of today India has a weapons-grade Pu stock of half a tonne (worth about 100 warheads), plus nearly twelve tonnes of reactor grade Pu (worth over 1,200 warheads). Surely, that should suffice for even for a much more conservative strategy. I do not believe we need more fissile material for deterrence purposes.

Thus, I feel that India should make every effort, consistent with sovereignty and national security, to reassure its neighbours and the world that it has no plans to exploit the deal to enlarge its arsenal beyond what is outlined in its nuclear doctrine document.

Big Empty Spot: "Recognition" and India's Nuclear Weapon Status

James F. Keeley

This paper will examine some issues arising from the US-India Joint Statement of July 18, 2005 (White House 2005). The question of how India should be treated in the context of this co-operative proposal raises basic issues for the nuclear non-proliferation regime, in suggesting an exception to the existing distinction, established in the NPT, between NWS and NNWS. Whether such an exception should be made, whether, if made, it should be regarded as a one-off or be rules-based, and what its contents should be are all matters of considerable disagreement. As a way of cutting through the potential implications, the paper will draw on the concept of recognition in international law. Although that concept is legal, it also has political and psychological aspects that are of possible use here.

Setting the General Problem

Following earlier Indian tests, a discussion occurred among some members of the international nuclear non-proliferation academic community over whether India should be termed a "nuclear weapon state." The question, which was arcane rather than unrealistic, concerned the political and legal implications of applying that term to a state that, while possessing nuclear weapons, was not one of the five designated NWS of the NPT. Would using this term give India a status, whether political or legal, that might be undesirable in this light, by indicating an acceptance or even a rewarding of its tests, with negative implications for the nuclear non-proliferation regime? To avoid complications in terminology, this paper shall adopt the convention of reserving the term NWS for those so designated under the NPT, and shall instead term India a "state with nuclear weapons" (SNW).[1] Therefore, though in terms of the NPT (for the states party to it) and in terms of domestic law in many states, India is often treated as an NNWS, it is a non-NPT NNWS that is an SNW. This is why things can get confusing. Adding India to the list of NWS is not at issue here; rather, the question is now how to handle it as a state with nuclear weapons as a matter of accepted fact, yet outside the NPT.

---

[1] The other term currently in use—"responsible State with advanced nuclear technology"—artfully avoids the weapons issue.

This old debate recalls two stories—one true and one fictional. The first story—the true one—concerns the US refusal, for over two decades, to recognize the People's Republic of China (PRC)[2] as the government of the Chinese state. This refusal, whether dictated initially merely by dislike compounded by the Korean War, or by a hope that the PRC's defeat of the Chinese Nationalist government might be reversed, allowed the US to deny the PRC certain advantages under its domestic law that would have followed on recognition, and to block it until the 1970s from taking the Chinese seat at the UN, including in the Security Council. Ultimately, however, the US found that the PRC was not going away, and would have to be dealt with, even if informally. The American refusal to recognize, however limited its ultimate political impact, nonetheless took on a symbolic importance, which could hamper not only the US and the PRC but also others trying to navigate between them. Ultimately, of course, a dialogue begun under President Nixon resulted in American recognition in 1978 (although with a continuation of the Taiwan anomaly). Now, the question of how to incorporate China constructively into the international system continues, but the mechanisms and approaches of exclusion have been replaced, in part at least, by mechanisms of inclusion.

The same problem is posed by India with respect to both the nuclear non-proliferation regime and the world political system. There are clear tensions between the political-technical-legal character of the first (and its peculiar discriminatory character) on the one hand and the political character of the second on the other. For the first, the nuclear non-proliferation regime, centered on the NPT, is based on a distinction between 5 designated NWSs, of which India is not one, and the remaining states, designated as NNWSs. While this regime is thus initially discriminatory between NWSs and NNWSs, negotiations to be undertaken in good faith under Article VI of the NPT are, in theory, to remove this discrimination at some unspecified future date. Within the NNWS category, the attendant safeguards system (INFCIRC/153) seeks to formally treat like actors in similar ways and on a technical-objective basis. This, of course, masks an initial political focus under a suitably technical-objective cover.[3] For the world political system, however, a cold-blooded view suggests that nuclear weapons are not going away

---

[2] The original "big empty spot" from which the title of this paper is derived.

[3] Initially, a primary concern for the NPT negotiators was with states with relatively strong nuclear-industrial capabilities, especially in Europe. The safeguards focus that developed was oriented to nuclear material, and thus to the larger nuclear-industrial states. This resulted in what many—including Canada—have complained is an unsuitable allocation of inspection efforts towards states, primarily Canada, Germany, and Japan, which present little or no actual proliferation threat.

anytime soon. Pending the Second Coming, or the Greek Kalends, it therefore makes a difference who has them. Politics is in part precisely about discriminating; for example, between those whom we might wish to include in the ranks of the great and good, and those whom we might wish to exclude even if we less formally acknowledge their influence. This is not a less principled or a more hypocritical undertaking than the first, merely one based on different principles. To think otherwise is similar to being shocked at finding gambling in Rick's *Café Américain*. The divorce between the non-proliferation discourse of non-discrimination, safeguards techniques applied on objective and technical criteria, and disarmament, and the political-strategic discourse of world order (for which non-proliferation concerns are only one factor), is a major difficulty both in analyzing the nuclear non-proliferation regime and in talking about it: certain things cannot be said in polite company.

The second, fictional, story is "The Monkey's Paw," the moral of which might be that we should be careful about what we wish for—we could get it in the worst possible way. In November 2004, a study prepared by the Canadian Department of Foreign Affairs for the Blix Commission suggested that efforts should be made to draw non-NPT states into "more comprehensive multilateral commitments and safeguards relating to their civilian nuclear cycles, including negotiation of a full-scope safeguards agreement and an Additional Protocol with the IAEA" (Foreign Affairs Canada 2004).

This, the study noted, would likely include separating civilian from military facilities, and would have to be done "in ways that did not imply acceptance of these countries as de facto nuclear weapons states" (Foreign Affairs Canada 2004). The proposal for US-India nuclear co-operation now presents this recommendation as a practical problem. Underlying this is the fundamental problem of how we are to categorize India, and how we are to approach it on the basis of that categorization. This leads us to the issue of recognition.

Recognition in International Law

Within the realm of international law, the theory and practice of recognition[4] may give us a means of thinking initially about both the nature of "recognition" of India's nuclear weapons status and some of its implications. In terms of this particular issue, of course, the question is more than simply legal. The political and symbolic aspects may be central, but still, legal aspects feed into these, and the conceptual vocabulary of the law might be of value even beyond the purely legal considerations.

---

[4] For a basic introduction, see, Malanczuk, cited here.

Even within international law, recognition is best approached as a political act with legal consequences. That is, it reflects primarily political calculations, but may have an impact in both domestic and international law and tribunals. Actors (states, governments, and others), situations, claims, etc. may all be recognized in international law. As an act of policy, states may grant or withhold recognition on the basis of "objective" criteria, or on the basis of a policy objective: granting recognition may signal acceptance of a fact; withholding recognition may not in one sense deny the fact, but may be a device to try to change it, or at least to put pressure on another by withholding certain advantages or benefits that would flow from recognition. In international law, recognition is an act by an individual state, which is free to grant it or withhold it as it sees fit. No international organization as such can confer recognition on a state or government, for example, even by granting membership in that organization. In the case of the NPT, however, status as either an NWS or an NNWS was negotiated and confirmed in the treaty as a collective act, and while states are free to join the treaty as NNWS or to withdraw from it on their own, changing status from an NNWS to an NWS requires a second collective act—amending the treaty. This complicates the comparison but does not void it.

Three sets of distinctions are of interest to us here: between the constitutive and the declaratory theories of recognition; between recognition *de jure* and recognition *de facto*; and between express and implied recognition.

The constitutive theory of recognition argues that recognition is necessary to create a legal fact; thus, in the absence of recognition, a government or a state would not exist in law. This theory holds best on the domestic level, where, for example, refusal to recognize an actor may deny it standing to sue in the courts of the non-recognizing state: no proper party may be before the court. Or, the acts of a recognized government might be granted validity in the courts of the state recognizing it, but those of an unrecognized government would not be upheld, as the government in question would not be held to exist. On the international level, this theory would seem applicable primarily to occasions where a situation or an actor is created in breach of international law: recognition (more particularly, recognition *de jure*) cures that breach. The declaratory theory argues, in contrast, that recognition merely acknowledges the existence of a situation and applies the consequences of that acknowledgement—it does not actually create the situation. This approach may be more applicable in international tribunals, but is not really applicable generally in domestic courts.

A distinction is also drawn on occasion between recognition *de jure* and recognition *de facto*. Recognition *de jure* confers a sense of legality or legitimacy, and perhaps also permanency. A government recognized *de jure* is the lawful or legitimate government, while a claim-of-title recognized *de jure* is one accepted as lawful. A government-recognized *de facto* may simply be the current government. A defective claim to territory, recognized *de jure*, has that defect cured; a *de facto* recognition, on the other hand, might merely acknowledge that a state controls a territory for the time being, but its legal right to do so is still in question. So, for example, by refusing to recognize *de jure* South Africa's former claims to the territory that is now the independent state of Namibia, the world community indicated that in its opinion the future legal status of the territory was still an open question. One might refuse recognition of a state's claim to territory; for example, under the Stimson Doctrine (applied to Japan's activities in Manchuria in the inter-war period), precisely in order to deny that state the fruits of aggression, effectively limiting its claimed legal rights and standing with respect to that territory.

Recognition may be express or implied. In the former case, a clear statement of recognition, with a clear intent to recognize, removes all doubt as to the intent of the actor recognizing and as to the resulting status of the actor, situation, or claim so recognized. In the latter case, however, recognition is inferred by the activities of the supposedly recognizing actor toward the actor, situation, or claim involved: are these such that they imply or could only be based on such recognition? The difficulty with implied recognition is that it may be possible for a state to disavow any intent to recognize regardless of its behaviour. It is possible to conduct many interactions with another state or government, for example, yet not to recognize it: the US could exchange table-tennis teams with the PRC, receive pandas for temporary exhibit in its zoos, talk to representatives of the PRC, and even open a liaison office in Beijing, without recognizing the PRC as the government of China.

India as an SNW

How might these distinctions apply to India in the nuclear case? If India was to sign the NPT as an NNWS, it would agree to the express, *de jure* status of a state without nuclear weapons under that treaty. It would be legally constituted as an NNWS participant in the treaty, with consequent implications for the reorientation of its nuclear program and facilities and the application of full-scope safeguards under INFCIRC/153, if not also the Additional Protocol (INFCIRC/540). On the other hand, if India was to sign as an NWS, it would take on the express, *de jure* status of a nuclear weapon state under the treaty: it would be legally constituted as an NWS under the terms of the treaty.

It is precisely the matter of NPT status that creates the basic problem of the India-US arrangement. Only five states qualify as NWS under the NPT: the US, the UK, the USSR (and Russia as its successor), France, and China. Article IX.3 defines a nuclear weapon state for the purposes of the NPT as one that manufactured and exploded a nuclear weapon or other nuclear explosive prior to January 1, 1967. All others are to be considered as NNWS, regardless of their actual or possible possession of nuclear weapons. Admitting additional states to the NWS category would require opening up the NPT to amendment, itself a dangerous and difficult process.[5]

It would also be seen as defeating the purpose of the treaty, sending the wrong signal to other states, and possibly undermining the broader nuclear non-proliferation regime. The fundamental argument here is over what considerations states would respond to in deciding to acquire or to continue to forego nuclear weapons. Some analysts contend that the impact would be limited, on the grounds that states make proliferation decisions based on local circumstances, not broader considerations. As against this, however, is the fear that current states outside the regime, or that may be developing weapons or a latent or breakout weapons capability within them, or other states within the regime that came in in good faith, could take special treatment of India as an insult, a model or a hope (du Preez and Duarte 2006; Huntley and Sasikumar 2006; Nunn 2006).

So, for example, on the breakup of the Soviet Union, considerable efforts were devoted to ensuring that the Ukraine was admitted to the NPT as an NNWS, and to getting it to give up what nuclear weapons remained on its soil. Italy referred explicitly to this limiting definition of an NWS in its statement attached to its signature of the NPT, declaring that "Any claim to belong to this category, and for any title, shall not be recognized by the Italian Government to other States, whether or not they have signed the Treaty." Japan noted that the NPT permits "only the present nuclear-

---

5 Amending the NPT, under the terms of Art. VIII.2, requires a majority of (a) all parties to the treaty, (b) including all the votes of the NWS party to the treaty, and (c) including the votes of all other parties to the treaty that are on the Board of Governors of the International Atomic Energy Agency as of the date of circulation of the proposed amendment.

weapon States to possess nuclear weapons," but linked this to future disarmament talks.[6]

However, even if states did not attach such statements to their signatures, they could still respond, if they believed that their interests were crucially challenged, by availing themselves of their right under Article X.1 to withdraw on three months' notice.

The enormous political, psychological, and legal consequences attending an explicit, *de jure,* and constitutive recognition of India as an NWS under the NPT effectively ensure that this will be most unlikely. It is worth noting, however, that an Indian signature of the NPT, whether or not as an NWS, would itself also be a singular reversal of a long-standing and fundamental Indian complaint about the treaty. Even during the negotiation of the NPT, India made it clear that it objected to the discrimination made explicit between the then-existing NWSs and NNWSs. Signing the NPT in *any* capacity would entail repudiating this principled objection—to India's disadvantage if as an NNWS, or to its advantage if as an NWS. Of course, if India adopts the NSG guidelines, which generally contain a full-scope safeguards requirement—though India would be exempted in this regard under US proposals—it would be required to apply full-scope safeguards to others while itself avoiding them. Thus, while India might succeed in dismantling that portion of the nuclear non-proliferation regime that it sees as unfairly discriminating against it, it would in return be accepting some degree of discrimination against others (Kimball 2006). India has no intention of signing the NPT as an NNWS, nor does it seek to join the treaty as an NWS. For its part, the US notes that it is not recognizing India as an NWS under the NPT (White House 2006).

The US tends to downplay the *de facto* and implicit aspect of its arrangement with India outside of the NPT. But whether or not one wishes to argue that *de facto* and at least implicit recognition has occurred in the legal sense, in the looser and in many ways more relevant political and psychological senses that conclusion is hard to avoid. The establishment of a separation plan prior to the development of a safeguards system for India's designated civilian nuclear sector makes sense only if India is being treated as possessing nuclear weapons. This implication is not avoided if the recognition is posed as *de facto* and implicit—and statements by the Indian Prime Minister make it clear that

---

[6] Declaration of January 28, 1969, para. 11. The list of parties to the NPT and their various statements upon signature, ratification, access, or adherence to the NPT are available at http://disarmament.un.org/TreatyStatus.nsf/.

India regards the Joint Statement and its implementation as effectively providing it with such recognition (India Prime Minister's Office 2006b).

But in what capacity, then, has India been "recognized"? The NPT presents only two choices in the NWS-NNWS dichotomy created in the NPT. What is the status of this dichotomy, and particularly of the NNWS category, beyond the NPT? A fundamental rule of treaty law is that if a treaty creates a new rule, that rule is binding only on the signatories of that treaty, not on non-signatories. By that fundamental rule, NNWS status as a legal category applies only within the NPT, not beyond it. If member states seek, for example in domestic legislation or in export practices, to draw others into the NPT in the NNWS category, or to treat them in terms similar to NNWSs, that is an indication of their policy or of their desire, not an obligation binding on non-signatories. One might attempt to argue that the dichotomy and the broad application of NNWS status has now entered customary law, and could therefore be binding even on non-parties. If so, however, the fact that India objected to the distinction even as it was being negotiated, refused to sign the NPT on this basis, and has been consistent in its protest since, would seem to qualify it for the "persistent objector" exception (Malanczuk 1997). One might also attempt to argue that the NPT, being so widely adhered to, is now an "objective" law binding even on non-signatories, but that could also be debated (Malanczuk 1997).

How should India be treated? Should it receive the same treatment as an NWS (which some statements seem to indicate is what it expects[7])? What of the implications of this for the NPT and the wider regime? One alternative to this quandary would have been to constructively exploit the ambiguity possible in a situation short of recognition. The US-PRC case demonstrates that a lot can go on short of even implicit recognition. Such an approach would not seek to resolve the Indian anomaly, but rather would embrace and preserve it. But creative non-recognition no longer seems to be on the table as an alternative. The political argument within the US, and by extension the question both between the US and India and between any US-Indian arrangement on the one hand and the nuclear

---

[7] E.g., "[W]e have virtually got all the benefits that go with being a Nuclear Weapon State without having the *de jure* status of a Nuclear Weapon State." India, Prime Minister's Office, "PM's Reply to the Lok Sabha debate on his US visit, August 3, 2005," http://pmindia.nic.in/speech/content4print.asp?id=160. The psychological aspect of this should not be underestimated. One is struck in various statements of the Indian prime minister by the sense of wounded pride aroused by India's previous treatment in the nuclear area. This is itself part of a broader sense that India's real and potential status as a global player has not received its due, and that this arrangement with the US is part of a desired remedying of this situation.

non-proliferation regime on the other, will likely be defined and assessed overwhelmingly as one of getting as close as possible to one or the other of the two mutually exclusive categories of the NPT.

Some supporters of the current non-proliferation regime may want to push toward the NNWS side as much as they can. The problem is further complicated by the tremendous investment that has gone into creating and detailing the NPT dichotomy in both international practice and national legislation. Some of this effort, arguably, has gone beyond a strict reading of the NPT itself (which permits safeguarded exports to non-parties). Even so, if the treaty provisions are themselves now a floor—a set of minimum requirements—in some sense, the generally applicable rules in bodies such as the NSG and in much domestic export control legislation have moved above this floor. Further, after much effort, the NSG itself moved to accept full-scope safeguards as its export standard to NNWSs, and got this accepted by NPT parties at the 1995 Review Conference. It is now being called upon to alter this standard.

Others may be willing to treat India as an NWS for certain purposes (effectively taking it at its word, and perhaps more), but insist that India accept *all* of the attendant burdens as well as the benefits. However, it would seem desirable from a regime perspective to avoid too close a parallel with the treatment of NWSs under the NPT in order to avoid rousing the envy and resentment of some NNWSs party to the NPT. There is a problem here both for India on the one hand, and opponents of the deal on the other: the more India is treated as an NWS that falls outside the NPT, the more problematic the result would be for the nuclear non-proliferation regime more generally if NNWS in the NPT are to be mollified. There must be a meaningful distinction, with some disadvantages to India attached as well as possibly some advantages, if this is to be avoided. Treating India as falling outside the NWS-NNWS dichotomy—treating it as an SNW—might allow an approach less disruptive of the NPT's categories and more constructive for the nuclear non-proliferation regime as a whole. If India is not an NWS, neither is it an NNWS: it is a State with Nuclear Weapons (SNW).

Parameters for SNW Status

What, then, might it mean to be an SNW—a third category in (or rather, outside of) a dichotomy? We may look at elements of the US-India statement as a possible prototype for such a category, supposedly brought closer to the nuclear non-proliferation regime yet not within the NPT.

Should the Indian case be treated as a one-of-a-kind exception—an anomaly to be resolved rather than welcomed—or as an instance of a broader, rule-based category? Currently, the US is seeking modification of NSG rules on an India-only basis. It is feared that exceptional treatment for India will invite efforts by others to seek exceptions for their favoured candidates as well. The consensus basis of decision in the NSG could favour this possibility if states trade support for future considerations. The possibility of additional exceptions, however, is not closed off by the development of a rules-based approach—unless those rules achieve that highest form of the art, an agreed, effective, objective, and technical category that in fact permits only the one case.

The basis for a limited Indian case, whether or not posed in terms of "objective" rules, would have to reside not only in the specific actions that India has taken or proposes to take, as cited in the US draft proposals for the NSG, though these certainly are helpful in setting criteria (Kimball 2006). It would need to be argued as well that the small set of states not party to the NPT, including those that have or are thought to have nuclear weapons, really form a leftover category grouped merely by what they are not. This is an internally heterogeneous group, and therefore one member cannot reasonably be expected to be treated automatically like another simply on the basis of this common membership in a residual set. There is no injustice in treating unlike cases differently. *Sui generis* treatment, within certain broad sets of considerations, would thus be the norm. These considerations would themselves be useful in drawing relevant distinctions. They could include: previous illegal behaviour; previous membership in and subsequent withdrawal from the NPT; possession (overt or suspected) of non-possession of nuclear weapons; potential or actual contribution to proliferation and non-proliferation, etc. Thus, not all states outside of the NPT would be treated as SNWs. Nor would all states outside of the NPT that have nuclear weapons: in part, a point of using the SNW category would be precisely to link these states positively to the non-proliferation regime more generally, even if they do not fall within the NPT. Others, outside of the NPT, even with nuclear weapons, might still be subjected to pressures to disarm.

If the US draft proposals are accepted, other states would be free to provide items that the US might not be willing to sell (Kimball 2006). But NSG guidelines still act as a floor of sorts, and so this must be factored into consideration of this point. Further, while they set some conditions governing sales (conditions that include requirements to be placed on recipients), the guidelines do not require any state to sell to all comers. Nor would they prevent a supplier state, through its bilateral civilian nuclear co-operation requirements, from placing more stringent conditions on its sales, including safeguards, contagion, retransfers, derived items, conditions for reprocessing or further enriching of fuel, and so on.

Among the various actions to be taken by India, as outlined in the Joint Statement and as noted in the US draft proposal to the NSG, some do not touch directly upon India's own status even as they bring it closer to the mainstream of desired practice *vis-à-vis* other states. These would seem to present clear gains for the non-proliferation regime in general, without raising the vexatious problem of recognition. Such measures include: supporting efforts to restrain the spread of sensitive nuclear technologies, such as enrichment and reprocessing; strengthening Indian export control legislation and mechanisms; observing Missile Technology Control Regime and NSG guidelines in India's own exports—this last, of course, having the peculiar effect noted above. Suggestions that India participate in the Proliferation Security Initiative have also been made. India has noted that it has certain concerns on this score (India Prime Minister's Office 2006a), but this need not preclude informal co-operation. Suggestions that India commit itself to supporting measures against Iran have aroused a strong response, as impinging on its foreign policy independence. Here again, however, informal co-operation may be possible, and India has in fact acted in conformity with the recent UN Security Council resolution sanctioning Iran (Anon 2007).

Among areas in which Indian action has been sought, promised, or forthcoming, however, there are those where the NWS-SNW distinction does come into question even though they are outside the NPT as such. The NWS have, with certain exceptions and variations, acted in these areas, so pressing India to conform to their broad standard raises the difficulty noted above. First, India has committed itself to continue its current unilateral moratorium on testing, but there are demands that it should sign the CTBT. India will resist pressure to sign the CTBT, and in light of US non-ratification the case to press it is less than overwhelming. (This could, in fact, be a device to put pressure for CTBT action on both India and the US.) Second, while India has committed itself to working with the US toward a Fissile Materials Cutoff Treaty—and the meaning of this seems fairly vague—some have demanded that India should end its fissile material production now, as the NWSs have done. Again, India has rejected this demand. The nature of its general grand scheme for nuclear energy, progressing toward a thorium cycle (India Prime Minister's Office 2005),[8] as well as any desire to increase the size of its nuclear arsenal, would seem to preclude such a shutdown.

---

[8] The plan would begin with the current power reactors, move to breeder reactors, and finally to a thorium-based fuel cycle, taking advantage of India's large thorium deposits.

There are, finally, those areas in which direct comparison with the treatment given to NWSs under the NPT and to NNWSs by nuclear exporters will be inevitable and unavoidable. Two major areas here are the separation plan and attendant safeguards by the IAEA, and some of the terms of any specific US-India nuclear co-operation agreement.

India has proposed a draft plan for the separation of civilian nuclear facilities from those in the non-civilian sector (India Department of Atomic Energy 2005). This terminology for the distinction is not adequate, however, given the peculiarities of that separation plan: provision of civilian nuclear power versus supply of a military sector is not the actual or sole basis of the division. It would be better to refer to an "open" sector that could receive foreign input and would be safeguarded, and a "reserved" or "closed" sector that would not be safeguarded.[9] The reserved sector in the Indian plan not only encompasses a military component but also seeks to protect from external influence its research and development activities and facilities deemed crucial for its long-term three-stage nuclear power plan. It may be feared regarding this last that, while external technology, etc. could be beneficial, the conditions and safeguards that would accompany it would be undesirable. The nature of this distinction, however, increases the size of the reserved sector, and feeds concerns (also found in the argument that India should agree to a cutoff in fissile materials production) that India could continue or even (through relieved pressure on its domestic uranium supplies) significantly increase its rate of production of fissile materials for weapons use (Mian et al. 2006; Tellis 2006).

The open sector would be subject to IAEA safeguards, including an Additional Protocol arrangement. (This last is seen as somewhat symbolic, given the separation plan and the non-full-scope safeguards resulting in the first place, but could at least give a window on the open sector.) Bits of information thus far available suggest that these would not simply be parallel, however, to those found in the voluntary arrangements between NWSs and the IAEA (India Department of Atomic Energy 2005). Taking the US-IAEA agreement as a point of comparison (US Department of State nd), under this agreement the US distinguishes between facilities eligible for the application of safeguards by the IAEA and those not eligible. Of the eligible set, the IAEA then chooses which it will actually apply safeguards to, though it can receive necessary design information and the like about the rest. The tremendous strain on IAEA resources

---

[9] The distinction then also raises the issue of the leakage of information and technology, if not of equipment and materials, from the open sector to the reserved sector.

that would flow from trying to safeguard all the eligible US facilities is a factor in this, but it also indicates the largely symbolic nature of the NWS safeguards. Crucially, the US retains the right to add facilities to, or withdraw them from, the eligible set.

A full parallel between the treatment given India and that given to NPT-NWS would lead us to expect a similar flexibility—something not to be desired. By comparison, it would appear that although India will (like the US) retain the right to determine which sector a facility falls into, it will accept safeguards in perpetuity on facilities in the open sector. A report in October 2006 suggests, however, that India may be "balking at the notion of permanent IAEA safeguards for its entire civilian nuclear sector" (Boese 2006). A later report indicates that India wants to avoid INFCIRC/66-type safeguards, under which "material imported or produced under safeguards" would remain under safeguards (Boese 2007).

Thus, any facilities initially declared in that set, and any subsequently added to it, will stay there. The result may be, depending on how the two sectors develop in the future, that a substantial portion of the Indian nuclear program comes under safeguard. While the addition of a significant number of additional facilities to the IAEA safeguards list may still strain its resources, it would also still be desirable to avoid the expedient adopted in the US case of having the agency merely choose a few from the eligible list. With sufficient additional agency resources, the entire set could be put under permanent safeguard. The combination of locked-in categories and full agency application of safeguards within the open sector would mark a significant practical and helpful distinction between India's treatment and that afforded to NWS. Further, if, for example, a contagion principle is applied to imported information, technology, equipment, and material, this would help to reinforce the Indian separation scheme. However, India has indicated a willingness to accept "campaign mode" safeguards at its Tarapur reprocessing facility for safeguarded material (India Department of Atomic Energy 2005).

Problematically, India has demanded (based on its experience with the Tarapur power reactor[10]) assurances from the US of a fuel supply, even if the US for some reason might itself cease supply, and the right to build up a fuel reserve to protect against supply disruptions. While this has an obvious impact on the terms of any US-India nuclear co-operation agreement, it is also linked to the broader safeguards issue. India's prime

---

[10] This reactor was, under the terms of the 1963 agreement with the US, to be supplied with US fuel only. Following the termination of US-India nuclear co-operation after the 1974 test, alternative fuel supplies—first from France and then from the USSR—had to be arranged and agreed upon between the US and India.

minister has stated that the offer of perpetual safeguards for the open sector is contingent on securing an international supply of fuel for these facilities for their lifetime (India Prime Minister's Office 2006a). The basic concern here would be whether such an assurance of supply would hold in the event of another Indian nuclear test. If the assurance was in the form of a sizeable stockpile held in India, the problem is obvious. It should be noted that current broadly phrased proposals for fuel supply assurances (in return for states foregoing reprocessing or enrichment) cover only commercial disruptions, not interruptions based on non-proliferation concerns. Even if India avoids being formally bound by a legal commitment not to conduct further testing, can it reasonably expect to be given essentially a free hand?

Finally, there are the terms of any specific US-India nuclear co-operation agreement. The US administration has committed itself to modify legislation—above all the requirement for full-scope safeguards—that would hinder nuclear trade with India, and has sought with some success to block proposed amendments to legislation enabling the Joint Statement, which would potentially kill such an agreement. But which US controls and rights, standard in its other co-operation agreements, will be applied and which might not? The fuel supply issue raises a problem in this regard, as the US typically reserves the right to cancel or suspend deliveries if a nuclear test occurs. As well, the US typically retains a right of consent not only to transfers of supplied and derived items to third parties, but also to any reprocessing or enrichment (or further enrichment) of supplied fuel. This might present the possibility of a significant impact on future Indian nuclear plans. India is reportedly seeking pre-approval treatment for reprocessing similar to that the US gives to Europe and Japan (Boese 2007). Failure to obtain such an assurance, in turn, presents an incentive to India to preserve a significant non-military but still reserved sector in which it might more freely produce fissile material.

Whether in its multilateral or its bilateral requirements, carrying out the Joint Statement will also present significant sequencing problems, as each side will want to ensure that vital commitments are carried out by the other before it performs key actions itself. For example, India would want to have all restrictions on it lifted before its designated facilities come under safeguards (India Prime Minister's Office 2005).

NWS-SNW: A Dime's Worth of Difference?

While the US correctly notes that it has not recognized India as an NWS under the terms of the NPT, and India has not sought this status, the US-

India agreement, if it goes through in its multilateral as well as its bilateral aspects, would nonetheless seem to be *de facto* and implicit recognition of India in a nuclear capacity. The separation plan requirement otherwise makes no sense. But what sort of capacity is this? It is suggested here that, rather than confining ourselves to thinking simply in terms of the binary and mutually exhaustive NWS-NNWS categories offered under the NPT, it might be useful to create a third category—the SNW. The implications of this include that the NWS-NNWS dichotomy would be reserved purely to states party to the NPT. As well, although now full-scope safeguards are accepted as the standard applied to NNWSs both within and outside the NPT, the new category would challenge this. The NPT requires safeguards on exports, including to states outside the treaty, and full-scope safeguards on exports to NNWSs within it. While the full-scope requirement continues within the NPT, it would no longer apply of necessity to states on the outside. That would be a matter of agreement among suppliers. (In this case, however, it would require positive agreement among NSG members to reduce the requirements for a non-party.)

Not all states outside the NPT would be SNWs, even those that actually have nuclear weapons. The category would be intended to provide a legal framework for a positive relationship between a specified state and the broader non-proliferation regime, outside of NPT membership. It would not imply that all non-NPT states would fall under its terms, nor would it preclude efforts to get at least some of these to enter the NPT as NNWSs. The key problem is whether a meaningful and acceptable distinction can be drawn between an SNW so intended and those states categorized under the NPT as NWSs. If this can be done, the nuclear non-proliferation regime might well emerge extended and strengthened in practical terms. If, however, the distinction is not convincingly made to the satisfaction, especially of some NNWSs currently under the NPT, considerable damage to the nuclear non-proliferation regime might well result without sufficient compensating gain. The technical terms of the distinction will not be settled until the safeguards and the nuclear co-operation agreements are signed. The response to these arrangements will be governed largely by political and psychological considerations, but their technical character may still be a factor in influencing how states respond.

India and the Obligations of Nuclear Weapon States

Ernie Regehr

India describes itself as, and aspires to be recognized as, a nuclear weapon state (NWS). Such formal recognition is not forthcoming, but the US-India deal on civilian nuclear co-operation would, if fully implemented, have the effect of treating India as if it were a NWS. This paper argues that, as a *de facto* nuclear weapon state (DNWS) seeking international cooperation in civilian nuclear programs, India should be willing to meet all NWS-defined disarmament commitments and obligations.

The NWS have themselves defined what is required of them to advance the internationally agreed objectives of global nuclear disarmament and nonproliferation. That is not to say that they have unfailingly complied with their own requirements, but they have in fact left little doubt about their obligations. Three essential agreements that set out NWS commitments and obligations are the NPT itself, the 1995 NPT Review Conference agreement on Principles and Objectives for nuclear non-proliferation and disarmament, and the 2000 NPT Review Conference agreement on "practical steps for the systematic and progressive efforts to implement article VI of the NPT."

NWS are under legal obligation, by virtue of Article VI of the NPT, to disarm. They have in fact, through Review Conference agreements, made unequivocal disarmament commitments − including the elimination of their nuclear arsenals. They have affirmed the central importance of ratification and entry-into-force of the CTBT, which cannot happen before all NWS, as well as other Annex II states (i.e. states with civilian nuclear technologies), have ratified it, and have committed to a moratorium on testing until that time. The NWS have committed to negotiating a FMCT and to observing voluntary, unilateral moratoria on the production of fissile materials for weapons purposes pending the entry into force of such a Treaty.

The NWS have undertaken not to threaten or use nuclear weapons against non-nuclear weapon state signatories to the NPT. They have agreed to reduce the operational status of their weapons and to diminish their role in their respective security policies. They have pledged to honour nuclear weapon-free zones (NWFZ). The NWS have agreed to place nuclear materials and facilities which are surplus to their security needs under permanent IAEA safeguards. They are under legal obligation (again by virtue of the NPT) not to assist non-nuclear weapon states in the acquisition of nuclear weapons. They have agreed to regular reporting on their nuclear arsenals and on their progress in meeting their acknowledged disarmament objectives.

NWS are far from full compliance with their extensive undertakings and obligations, but it is possible to construct a scenario in which India's accession to *de facto* NWS status could increase pressure on NWS to live up to their disarmament responsibilities. If India, in deference to NWS disarmament commitments, were to become a leading disarmament advocate and enter into co-operative arrangements with even some NWS to aggressively promote the implementation of the NPT Chapter VI disarmament agenda, it could mean a new injection of energy into the nuclear nonproliferation, arms control and disarmament agenda. India finds itself at a compelling starting point inasmuch as it holds a number of progressive disarmament positions. Besides following what is in many ways a model nuclear doctrine of minimum deterrence (allowing, for the moment, for the oxymoron of a model nuclear doctrine), given that its weapons are not routinely on active deployment, and certainly not on any alert status under normal conditions, and given also that it is a strong rhetorical advocate for nuclear abolition, India is in a position to challenge NWS to act.

Thus, before the NSG acts on any Indian exceptions to nonproliferation regulations, the international community would do well to seek from India a clear indication of how it intends, as a *de facto* NWS, to meet the commitments and obligations that apply to NWS and, indeed, how it intends to engage the NWS and DNWS in developing practical measures to implement the disarmament agenda and to move toward India's stated goal of universal, nondiscriminatory disarmament.

India as a De Facto Nuclear Weapon State

India is not a NWS in the context of the NPT, but it obviously is a nuclear weapon state inasmuch as it has nuclear weapons and has a publicly articulated nuclear use doctrine as part of its national security apparatus. And while India will not be admitted as a NWS under the NPT, the US-India proposal to alter civilian nuclear co-operation rules and practices regarding India would, if fully implemented,

> treat India in much the same way as the five original nuclear-weapon states by exempting it from meaningful international nuclear inspections. It is a virtual endorsement of India's

nuclear weapon status. This outcome should not be unconditionally accepted, but critically appraised. (Arms Control Association 2006)

In other words, the deal recognizes the reality of *de facto* nuclear weapon states (DNWS) and, well before the US-India deal, analysts were exploring the idea of a "form of associate membership" in the NPT for the current non-signatories, all of which are DNWS "under a separate, freestanding agreement or protocol" (Cohen and Graham Jr. 2004).

Cohen and Graham argue that such an arrangement would recognize a reality without legitimizing nuclear weapons arsenals that are unambiguously at variance with the global norm that the NPT articulates. But in formally recognizing the reality of DNWS, those three states,[1] like the recognized NWS states, should be called on to "observe their half of the NPT bargain and work toward the ultimate elimination of nuclear weapons" (Cohen and Graham Jr. 2004). In other words, to be treated as a NWS means taking on the obligations of a NWS, which Cohen and Graham say includes, at a minimum, ratification of the CTBT, deeper cuts in stockpiles, legally binding negative security assurances (NSA), and the creation of a FMCT.

These are all essential and priority NWS obligations and commitments, but the list is much longer. The non-proliferation regime makes certain demands on the NWS, and the NWS makes certain commitments, but the NWS may meet those demands and live up to those commitments only to limited and varying degrees, so it is relevant to ask whether this state that is to be welcomed as a *de facto* member to the acknowledged nuclear weapons club will be amenable to meeting the demands and commitments of all NWS or whether it will simply expand the company of the recalcitrant.

The White House has insisted that the objective of the deal is to bring India fully into the nuclear non-proliferation regime and thus to "receive the benefits and accept all the responsibilities of the world's leading states with advanced nuclear technology," and that India would thus "assume the same responsibilities and practices as other countries with advanced nuclear programs" (US State Department 2005a).

The US under-secretary of state for political affairs, Nicholas Burns (US State Department 2005b), said at the time that the arrangements "commit India to comply with standards comparable to those of NPT signatory

---

[1] India, Israel, Pakistan; North Korea is a separate case as an NPT signatory that may now be on a (slow) path back to compliance with its NPT obligations.

countries" (meaning, obviously, NWS signatories). He said that the steps India has agreed to "are the same practices that all of us employ...." Burns insisted that the agreement does not recognize India as an NWS:

> This is all about nuclear power. It's not about nuclear weapons... [T]here's nothing in this about nuclear weapons. By taking this decision, we are not recognizing India as a nuclear weapons state. We are simply opening up a channel in order to cooperate on a commercial basis and a technological basis on nuclear power itself and that's a very important distinction.

Burns (US State Department 2005b) says it is "India's decision to make" as to whether it joins the NPT and that he "would never give advice to a country publicly"—forgetting apparently that Security Council Resolution 1172 (UNSC United Nations 1998) was quite free with public advice in that it "urges India and Pakistan, and all other States that have not yet done so, to become Parties to the Treaty on the Non-Proliferation of Nuclear Weapons and to the Comprehensive Nuclear Test Ban Treaty without delay and without conditions."

The responsibilities of NWS are defined by the NPT as well as by the decisions and commitments made through the NPT Review Conferences, held every five years, and the UN Security Council. In particular, the 1995 Review and Extension Conference (RevCon) and the 2000 RevCon reached significant agreements that expand on the obligations of NWS. In other words, by the treaties they have joined and the documents they have signed on to, and by the consensus they have joined, the NWS have themselves defined their obligations.

None of this is controversial or resisted by India. In a joint statement by President Bush and Prime Minister Manmohan Singh (White House 2005), Prime Minister Singh declared India to be "ready to assume the same responsibilities and practices and acquire the same benefits and advantages as other leading countries with advanced nuclear technology, such as the US." However, when Senator Byron Dorgan introduced an amendment to that effect in the US legislation, it was rejected. In defence of his amendment, Dorgan said:

> my amendment requires the President to determine that India has committed itself to pursuing negotiations on measures directed at reducing nuclear stockpiles and eventually eliminating nuclear weapons. These are the same commitments, the very same commitments our country has

made, the same commitments other nation states which have signed the nonproliferation treaty have made. So I believe it is appropriate that if we have this agreement with India dealing with the issue of nuclear weapons, they should be under the same obligations we are under. Even though they have not signed the nonproliferation treaty, we have. We have obligations under that treaty. They should accept the obligations under that treaty, in my judgment, even though they have not yet signed it (US Consulate in Chennai 2006).

In the meantime, India still faces a particular set of obligations and demands by virtue of Resolution 1172. That resolution imposes obligations based on the understanding that India is a NNWS as defined in the context of the NPT. Obviously, if India were to be accepted as a DNWS it could no longer be expected to meet the obligations of UNSC 1172. Resolution 1172 (1998) calls on India and Pakistan "to cease development of ballistic missiles capable of delivering nuclear weapons." That India has paid this sanction scant attention is clear, and is illustrated by the Indian Defence Ministry's November 10, 2006 announcement that it had that day test-fired the medium-range nuclear-capable Prithvi missile with a range of up to 300 kilometres – three days after Pakistan tested its nuclear-capable Ghauri missile (Mishra 2006). In that case, it would be incumbent on the Security Council to specifically absolve India of its obligations under 1172—a move that would then require a decision on Pakistan. Would Pakistan be granted the same exemption, or would the Security Council decide to bless an India-only exemption and thus introduce another level of double standards into the non-proliferation regime? There is not much suspense involved in the question; in fact, we can be sure that the Security Council will simply ignore the issue, leaving the US to remain sanguine in the face of Indian and Pakistani violation of a Security Council resolution while calling Iran's violation of another resolution a global crisis.

The US legislation is clear that the arrangement with India is to be India-specific. The final version contains no Senate inclusion of a specific statement that any NSG exemption for India would not permit an exception for another NNWS. However, the exemption described is specifically for India. It also calls for an NSG consensus decision on any other exemption (Squassoni and Parillo 2006).

Behind this discussion of India as a DNWS and its NWS obligations is the question of Canada's policy toward nuclear co-operation with India as a DNWS. The following argues that any Canadian civilian nuclear co-operation with India, with its explicit acknowledgement of India as a

DNWS, should first require full Indian acceptance of the commitments and obligations of the NWS. The fact that NWS are themselves not fully in compliance with their commitments and obligations should not be regarded as grounds for absolving India of those commitments and obligations. In other words, the Canadian requirement should be strict compliance and a willingness on the part of India to become a champion of strict compliance among all DNWS and NWS.

India's Nuclear Forces and Doctrine

Robert Norris and Hans Kristensen (2005) estimate India's current arsenal at forty to fifty "assembled nuclear warheads." That force could expand over the next half-dozen years to as many as three to four hundred warheads and India is in the process of establishing a strategic command to manage land-based, maritime, and airborne nuclear forces.

On 4 January 2003, India's Cabinet Committee on Security (CCS), headed by Prime Minister Vajpayee, released details of a review of the "operationalization of India's nuclear doctrine." The doctrine can be summarized as follows:

(i)   Building and maintaining a credible minimum deterrent

(ii)   A posture of "No First Use": nuclear weapons will only be used in retaliation against a nuclear attack on Indian territory or on Indian forces anywhere

(iii)   Nuclear retaliation to a first strike will be massive and designed to inflict unacceptable damage

(iv)   Nuclear retaliatory attacks can only be authorized by the civilian political leadership through the Nuclear Command Authority

(v)   Non-use of nuclear weapons against non-nuclear weapon states

(vi)   However, in the event of a major attack against India, or Indian forces anywhere, by biological or chemical weapons, India will retain the option of retaliating with nuclear weapons

(vii)   A continuance of strict controls on export of nuclear and missile-related materials and technologies, participation in the Fissile Material Cutoff Treaty negotiations, and continued observance of the moratorium on nuclear tests

(viii)   Continued commitment to the goal of a nuclear weapons-free world, through global, verifiable, and non-discriminatory nuclear disarmament (India Cabinet Committee on Security 2003).

A Nuclear Command Authority headed by the Prime Minister is the only body that can authorize the use of nuclear weapons.

In 1999, India's National Security Advisory Board released a draft report on nuclear doctrine as a discussion document. While the document was not formally accepted by the government, nothing in the CCS statement is sharply at odds with the draft, and the latter indicates that India's strategic analysis community reflects a healthy sense of both the dangers and the limited military utility of nuclear weapons.

The draft report begins with a welcome recognition of the threat of weapons of mass destruction and criticism of NWS first-use policies, which, it says, "constitute a threat to peace, stability and sovereignty of states." It includes the novel argument that the 1995 permanent extension of the NPT "legitimized" the possession of nuclear weapons "on a selective basis," and, inasmuch as it accepts the ongoing reliance of some on nuclear weapons, it represents the "virtual abandonment of nuclear disarmament."

In claiming the need for an "effective, credible nuclear deterrence and adequate retaliatory capability should deterrence fail," the draft doctrine sets out "a doctrine of credible minimum nuclear deterrence" that is based on a "retaliation only" posture. First use is thus rejected, as is use against NNWS not aligned with a NWS. At the same time, it states that India will maintain "highly effective conventional military capabilities" in order "to raise the threshold of outbreak both of conventional military conflict as well as that of threat or use of nuclear weapons." As is generally the pattern, the possession of nuclear weapons is not regarded as permitting the relaxation of conventional preparedness.

The draft doctrine states that "global, verifiable, and non-discriminatory nuclear disarmament is a national security objective" and promises India's continuing pursuit of a "nuclear weapon-free world at an early date." It goes on to call for "an international treaty banning first use" and says India will "work for internationally binding unconditional negative security assurances by nuclear weapon states to non-nuclear weapon states."

The essentials of the doctrine were repeated by India's disarmament ambassador in the Conference on Disarmament (CD) in August 2006:

> India's nuclear doctrine is based on a posture of no-first use
> and non-use of nuclear weapons against non-nuclear-weapon
> states. Nuclear weapons will only be used in retaliation against
> a nuclear attack on Indian territory or on Indian forces
> anywhere. We have, thus, provided the assurances to non-
> nuclear-weapon States. India is prepared to enshrine its
> commitments in legally binding instruments or arrangements
> (Prasad 2006c).

Both a RAND study of India's emerging nuclear posture (Tellis 2001) and a *Jane's Intelligence Review* report (Rethinaraj 2002) say that India's interest is in a nuclear arsenal that is not operationally deployed but is strategically significant. Both refer to a retaliatory capacity that would be available in a matter of hours to weeks—with the *Jane's* report suggesting that pressures will grow on India to develop and maintain a fully deployed nuclear arsenal.

To the extent that an international community that has formally decided that no nuclear weapons are ultimately acceptable, and that has made legally binding treaty commitments to eliminate all nuclear arsenals, can incorporate a "progressive" nuclear doctrine, much of India's approach deserves to be emulated by other DNWS and by NWS on the way to complete nuclear disarmament. That is not to say that India is fully committed to all of the obligations and commitments of the NWS; the following section reviews those basic commitments and India's stance toward them.

Nuclear Weapon State Obligations and Indian Compliance

Disarmament

The obligations are clear and unambiguous. The NPT Article VI requirement to disarm was reaffirmed in the 1995 RevCon Decision 2 on "Principles and Objectives for Nuclear Non-Proliferation and Disarmament." NWS reaffirmed their commitment "to pursue in good faith negotiations on effective measures relating to nuclear disarmament" (para 3) and to a "program of action" (para 4) that includes "the determined pursuit by the nuclear-weapon States of systematic and progressive efforts to reduce nuclear weapons globally, with the ultimate goals of eliminating those weapons, and by all States of general and complete disarmament under strict and effective international control."

Those commitments were, of course, reinforced by the final document of the 2000 RevCon, which, in outlining practical steps to implement Article VI, agrees to "an unequivocal undertaking by the nuclear weapon States to accomplish the total elimination of their nuclear arsenals leading to nuclear disarmament to which all States parties are committed under Article VI" (Part I, para 15.6). In addition, states agreed to the need for a subsidiary body on nuclear disarmament within the Conference on Disarmament (para 15.4) and agreed to a number of specific interim disarmament measures (para 15.9), including:

(i)   Further unilateral reductions in nuclear arsenals

(ii)   Reductions in non-strategic nuclear weapons

(iii)   Engagement of all nuclear-weapon states in disarmament leading to the total elimination of their nuclear weapons

India's rhetorical commitment to total nuclear disarmament is unambiguous. The CCS (2003) statement on nuclear doctrine confirms India's "continued commitment to the goal of a nuclear weapon-free world, through global, verifiable and non-discriminatory nuclear disarmament."

When Prime Minister Singh visited South Africa in October 2006, South African President Thabo Mbeki pledged his country's support within the NSG for the accommodations sought for the US-India civilian nuclear co-operation deal. Notably, the two leaders also declared their "unwavering commitment...to the goal of the complete elimination of nuclear weapons in a comprehensive, universal, non-discriminatory and verifiable manner," declaring also that they favour nuclear weapons elimination within a specified time frame (Khare 2006b). It is this support for a specified time frame that separates India's posture from that of the NWS, and it is a commitment that India as a DNWS should press on them.

Ashley Tellis (2001) has predicted Indian restraint in its armament program, but premised as much on economic restraint as on posture planning: "Pakistan is likely to respond to continued Indian nuclearization with even more intense efforts of its own, which could in turn precipitate Indian counter-reactions. Fortunately, relatively strong economic constraints suggest that the nuclear build-up on both sides will generally be slow."

US legislation includes a number of policy statements that outline some reasonably strongly worded disarmament principles and assertions, but the policy section of the legislation has been declared by the president to be advisory rather than binding (on the grounds that it is the prerogative of the president to conduct the nation's foreign affairs).

Currently, US legislation

(i)   Supports engagement of India in the interests of strengthening its non-proliferation policy.

(ii)   States support for NPT and opposition to weapons development and calls for elimination of South Asian nuclear arsenals.

(iii)   Calls for a fissile material production moratorium for India, Pakistan, and China.

(iv)   Calls for support for other non-proliferation activities such as the PSI, Australia Group, Wassenaar, and prevention of Iran's acquisition of nuclear weapons (Squassoni and Parillo 2006).

India has of course always defended its acquisition of nuclear weapons as the actions of "a responsible nuclear power":

> We are fully conscious of the immense responsibilities that come with the possession of advanced technologies, both civilian and strategic. While we are determined to utilize our indigenous resources and capabilities to fulfill our national interests, we are doing so in a manner that is not contrary to the larger goals of nuclear non-proliferation. India will not be a source of proliferation-sensitive technologies...We will remain faithful to this approach, as we have been for the last several decades. We have done so despite the well-known glaring examples of proliferation, which have directly affected our security interests (Singh 2004).

The Indian external affairs minister's 2005 address (Singh 2005) articulates an overall and long-standing commitment to disarmament:

> India has an abiding interest in non-proliferation of Weapons of Mass Destruction not just for its own security but for peace and security of the world at large. It is now little remembered that India was amongst the initiators of the proposal for an international instrument to prevent the proliferation of nuclear weapons. We held, however, that such an instrument should involve not only a commitment by non-nuclear weapon States to abjure nuclear weapons but also a commitment from those in possession of nuclear weapons to cease the further production of fissile material for weapon purposes and to move towards complete elimination of nuclear weapons within a time-bound framework. The Treaty, as it eventually emerged,

unfortunately addressed only one part of the proliferation challenge.

During Prime Minister Rajiv Gandhi's tenure, India again took a major initiative in 1988 in presenting an action plan for the eventual and complete elimination of nuclear weapons in a time-bound manner. However, this practical and non-discriminatory proposal did not find favour with those possessing nuclear weapons arsenals.

The end of the Cold War, bringing with it an end to the nuclear confrontation between the two superpowers, once again presented a unique opportunity to move forward in the direction of reducing and eliminating nuclear weapons. These hopes have, however, been belied and instead of progressive steps toward nuclear disarmament, there has been, in general, a move to reassert the primacy of nuclear weapons in the security calculus of states, especially those with the largest nuclear arsenals. New doctrines and justification for use of nuclear weapons have been developed. Such an attitude feeds and strengthens the belief that nuclear weapons are a currency of power....

...Article VI commits the parties to the Treaty to pursue negotiations to bring about eventual global nuclear disarmament. India is not only committed to commencing negotiations for a nuclear weapons convention, it is also the only nuclear weapon state ready to do so.

The theme of non-discrimination is prominent in Indian disarmament commitments and was regularly included in Indian statements at the CD:

[W]e remain ready to engage and cooperate on the basis of equality, in all multilateral consultations, to develop such an effective framework, and to bring about a stable, genuine and lasting non-proliferation of weapons of mass destruction. Our eventual goal must remain the complete elimination of such weapons (Singh 2005).

India shares the belief that the very existence of nuclear weapons, and of their possible use or threat of their use, poses a threat to humanity. India has remained committed to the goal of a nuclear-weapon free world, to be achieved through global, verifiable and nondiscriminatory nuclear disarmament.

> India's resolution in the General Assembly on a "Convention on the Prohibition of the Use of Nuclear Weapons," first presented in 1982, requests the Conference on Disarmament to commence negotiations for an international convention prohibiting the use or threat of use of nuclear weapons under any circumstances. The resolution reflects India's belief that a multilateral, universal and binding agreement prohibiting the use or threat of use of nuclear weapons would contribute to the mitigation of the nuclear threat as an important interim measure. It would also help create the climate for negotiations leading to the elimination of nuclear weapons, thereby strengthening international peace and security.

> Trust can only be restored through a reaffirmation of the unequivocal commitment of all nuclear weapon States to the goal of complete elimination of nuclear weapons (Prasad 2006a).

As a *de facto* NWS that is not a signatory to the NPT, India does not consider itself bound by the treaty's Article VI disarmament obligations. For NWS these are legally binding obligations, confirmed as such by the 1996 World Court opinion, to enter into and conclude negotiations leading to the disarmament that Article VI mandates. While India's rhetorical commitment to nuclear disarmament, including the total elimination of nuclear arsenals, is clear and welcome and is even a model that the NWS would do well to emulate, without legally binding obligations it has the character of a national option. For example, India's approach to the CTBT and FMCT indicates that India regards these imperatives as options rather than obligations.

CTBT

At the 1995 RevCon, NWS joined all other states party to the NPT in agreeing to CD negotiations "on a universal and internationally and effectively verifiable Comprehensive Test Ban Treaty no later than 1996" and to "exercise utmost restraint" pending its entry into force (Decision 2, para 4[a]).

After the treaty was successfully negotiated, at the 2000 RevCon all states party to the NPT agreed on "the importance and urgency of signatures and ratifications, without delay and without conditions and in accordance with constitutional processes, to achieve the early entry into force of the Comprehensive Nuclear Test Ban Treaty." They also agreed on "a moratorium on nuclear-weapon-test explosions or any other nuclear explosions pending entry into force of that Treaty" (Part I, paras 15.1 and 2).

The CCS nuclear doctrine statement (India Cabinet Committee on Security 2003) promised "continued observance of the moratorium on nuclear tests." Similarly, in the July 2005 India-US agreement, India also promises to "continue its unilateral moratorium on nuclear testing" (US State Department 2005a). However, as the Federation of American Scientists (2002) put it, "despite promoting a test ban treaty for decades," India did not support the UN General Assembly resolution endorsing the CTBT. The FAS report continues:

> India objected to the lack of provision for universal nuclear disarmament "within a time-bound framework." India also demanded that the treaty ban laboratory simulations. In addition, India opposed the provision in Article XIV of the CTBT that requires India's ratification for the treaty to enter into force, which India argued was a violation of its sovereign right to choose whether it would sign the treaty. In early February 1997, Foreign Minister Gujral reiterated India's opposition to the treaty, saying that "India favors any step aimed at destroying nuclear weapons, but considers that the treaty in its current form is not comprehensive and bans only certain types of tests.

In other words, India has found a way of avoiding a legally binding commitment against further testing, on the declared grounds that the commitment doesn't go far enough. But in a 1999 interview, Foreign Minister Jaswant Singh was rather more frank about his government's approach to the CTBT:

> Our stand on the CTBT has been clear. In 1996, we decided that we could not accept the CTBT because it was not consistent with India's national security interest. Over the decades, successive governments took necessary steps to safeguard India's nuclear option. In 1996, it was clear to all that subscription to the CTBT at that time would have limited India's nuclear potential at an unacceptably low level. After conducting the nuclear tests of May 1998, to validate and update our technology, we have ensured the credibility of our nuclear deterrent into the foreseeable future; our scientists are now confident of conducting sub-critical tests, as also other non-explosive R&D [research and development] activity necessary for the purpose. That is why we declared a voluntary moratorium. This, in essence, meets the basic obligations of the CTBT.

The minister's case against ratification at that point is linked to international responses to the 1998 tests:

> We also announced a willingness to convert this undertaking into a *de jure* obligation. Clearly, this could not be done in a political vacuum. A positive environment had to be created. In reaction, a number of countries decided to impose restrictive economic measures on India. We have conveyed our disappointment at these actions (Singh 1999).

The implication here is that the US-India deal, if other states concur, would be significant in creating the "positive environment" needed to persuade India to "convert" its voluntary moratorium on testing into "a *de jure* obligation," i.e., ratification of the CTBT. That in turn suggests it would be reasonable to make CTBT ratification one of the prerequisites to civilian co-operation. It is an approach supported by Norwegian Foreign Minister Jonas Gahr Store, who told reporters that India's signing of the CTBT would be "a very positive step" that might facilitate Norway's support for India in the NSG (Anon 2006b).

US legislation does not make civilian nuclear co-operation conditional on India's ratifying the CTBT, but it restricts the Atomic Energy Act (AEA) requirement that the US terminate nuclear exports to a NNWS that has tested a nuclear device to tests carried out before July 18, 2005—this legislation would mean that co-operation would end in the event of another Indian test (Squassoni and Parillo 2006). In the meantime, "India has continued to observe a moratorium on nuclear explosive tests" (Prasad 2006a).

FMCT

Through the 1995 RevCon, the NWS joined the consensus of all states party to the NPT to agree on "the immediate commencement and early conclusion of negotiations on a non-discriminatory and universally applicable convention banning the production of fissile material for nuclear weapons or other nuclear explosive devices" (Decision 2, para 4[b]). The same call was reiterated at the 2000 RevCon, when again the NWS agreed with all other states party to the NPT on

> the necessity of negotiations in the Conference on Disarmament on a non-discriminatory, multilateral, internationally and effectively verifiable treaty banning the production of fissile material for nuclear weapons or other nuclear explosive devices in accordance with the statement of the Special Coordinator in 1995 and the mandate contained

therein, taking into consideration both nuclear disarmament and nuclear non-proliferation objectives. The Conference on Disarmament is urged to agree on a programme of work which includes the immediate commencement of negotiations on such a treaty with a view to their conclusion within five years (Part I, para 15.3).

All five NWS have halted production of fissile material for weapons purposes, although China has not formally declared a moratorium.[2]

India has to date refused to join a moratorium on the production of fissile materials for weapons purposes. The government's CCS statement (2003) promised "participation in the Fissile Material Cutoff Treaty negotiations." Earlier, the foreign minister had made the same commitment:

> We have, after the tests last year, announced our readiness to engage in multilateral negotiations in the Conference on Disarmament n Geneva for a non-discriminatory and verifiable treaty to ban future production of fissile materials for nuclear weapon purposes. This decision was taken after due consideration, which included an assessment of time frames for negotiations and entry into force of an FMCT. At this stage, India cannot accept a voluntary moratorium on production of fissile materials. Let me add that FMCT negotiations are a complex exercise. It will be important, therefore, as we go along to constantly monitor the pace, direction and content of these negotiations (Singh 1999).

The July 2005 India-US agreement does not include a moratorium, and promises only to work with the US "for the conclusion of a multilateral Fissile Material Cut Off Treaty" (White House 2005). Matthew Bunn and Anthony Wier (2006) assess the deal's implications for India and fissile material as follows:

> India, Pakistan, Israel, and North Korea, however, are still producing plutonium, HEU, or both for weapons use. In the U.S.-India nuclear deal negotiated over the past year, India agreed to support negotiation of an FMCT (a promise without much bite, since such negotiations are going nowhere and India did not promise to sign or ratify such an agreement if it was ever completed). But India was unwilling to stop producing additional weapons material, either immediately or

---

[2] There is broad agreement among analysts that China has halted production, even though it has not declared a moratorium.

at any specified time in the future; indeed, India insisted on leaving so many of its reactors outside of international safeguards that it would have the option, if it so chose, to drastically increase production of weapons plutonium.

This issue promises to be contentious in the ongoing international discussions on nuclear co-operation with India. The US legislation declares that the policy of the US aims to achieve a moratorium on the production of fissile material for nuclear explosive purposes by India, Pakistan, and the PRC (Squassoni and Parillo 2006). The same goes for a negotiated FMCT, but neither is made a condition of the nuclear co-operation deal. Whether others, at the NSG, for example, seek to make it a condition remains to be seen.

It is clear from the Indian critics of the deal that ongoing production of fissile materials for weapons purposes is regarded as a fundamental security requirement. Rajiv Sikri, a former foreign service official, criticizes the Hyde Act as giving the US too much leeway in monitoring uranium use and calls "for India to accelerate its efforts to more efficiently mine existing uranium deposits in India, to step up prospecting for new deposits, and to actively explore possibilities of getting uranium from non-NSG members (Sikri 2006)."

Canada, of course, has a special interest in India's fissile materials production since the Canadian-supplied CIRUS reactor and other power generating reactors based on the CANDU design are all to be excluded from IAEA inspections and thus all remain available for continued production of fissile material for weapons purposes, in ongoing violation of the original deal with Canada (notwithstanding the Indian External Affairs Minister's assertion that "India's nuclear programme, civilian or strategic, has not violated any international obligations" (Singh 2005)). Leonard Spector, the deputy director of the Monterey Institute Center for Nonproliferation Studies writes:

> Although India agreed to shut down the reactor in 2010, it can continue to use the unit to produce roughly a bomb's worth of plutonium for nuclear weapons each year until then.... India has also kept six nuclear electric power reactors [based on Canada's CANDU technology] off the civilian list [meaning they will not be subject to IAEA inspections and will thus be available for production of fissile material for weapons purposes].... India is keeping these six CANDUs in its strategic program because they can be operated to produce many bombs' worth of high-quality plutonium. The material can be used either directly in nuclear weapons or to fuel

breeder reactors that can produce more and even better-quality plutonium for weapons. Indeed, in a statement to the *Indian Express* last February, Anil Kakodkar, chairman of the Indian Atomic Energy Commission, openly declared that the reactors were being held back from inspection because they were needed for India's "security" and for maintaining India's "minimum credible deterrent."...[Canada] can demand [that]...in exchange for agreeing to end the NSG embargo...every reactor based predominantly on Canadian technology must be placed under IAEA inspection (Spector 2006).

The US legislation does not impose any firm requirements on India regarding restrictions on fissile material production for weapons purposes. It calls on India to work "actively" for the "early" conclusion of an FMCT. In the policy (i.e., advisory) section, the legislation bans US co-operation on enrichment and reprocessing, as well as on heavy water materials, equipment, and technology, unless it supports multilateral or bilateral fuel cycle co-operation, and as long as it does not improve India's ability to produce weapons or fissile materials for weapons (Squassoni and Parillo 2006). But, according to a 2006 report of the International Panel on Fissile Materials, changed NSG guidelines with regard to India – i.e., giving it access to foreign sources of uranium – would give India the capacity to accumulate enough plutonium for an arsenal of more than 300 nuclear warheads within a decade—an arsenal to rival or exceed those of the UK, France, and China (Mian et al. 2006).

In the meantime, India continues to declare its support for an FMCT:

> We are ready to participate in negotiations, in this Conference, on a non-discriminatory, multilateral and internationally and effectively verifiable treaty banning the production of fissile material for nuclear weapons or other nuclear explosive devices (Prasad 2006a).

> India continues to believe that any treaty banning the production of fissile material must be non-discriminatory: it must stipulate the same obligations and responsibilities for all States. While the nature, extent and mechanisms for verification shall no doubt be determined during the negotiations, we believe that an FMCT should incorporate a verification mechanism in order to provide the assurance that all States party to it are complying with their obligations under the Treaty...An FMCT must be a treaty for banning the future production of fissile material for nuclear weapons or other nuclear explosive devices (Prasad 2006b).

India clearly accepts the formal commitment the NWS have made, in 1995 and 2000, to pursue an FMCT, but so far refuses to join others and accept the further commitment to halt all production of fissile materials for weapons purposes in anticipation of successful negotiation of an FMCT.

Negative Security Assurances

At the 1995 RevCon, nuclear weapon states not only committed not to use or threaten to use nuclear weapons against NNWS, but they agreed to at least consider making that commitment legally binding:

> Noting United Nations Security Council resolution 984 (1995), which was adopted unanimously on 11 April 1995, as well as the declarations of the nuclear-weapon States concerning both negative and positive security assurances, further steps should be considered to assure non-nuclear-weapon States party to the Treaty against the use or threat of use of nuclear weapons. These steps could take the form of an internationally legally binding instrument (Decision 2, para 8).

At the same time, some of the NWS—notably the US, Russia, and France—have through public statements and published policies qualified that commitment, to indicate use or threatened use of nuclear weapons in response to certain non-nuclear threats emanating from NNWS.

India makes an NSA declaration in its CCS statement (2003), saying its doctrine includes the "non-use of nuclear weapons against non-nuclear weapon states." But it immediately qualifies that commitment: "However, in the event of a major attack against India, or Indian forces anywhere, by biological or chemical weapons, India will retain the option of retaliating with nuclear weapons." Nevertheless, India does continue to support the pursuit of legally binding NSA:

> An agreement by Nuclear Weapon States ruling out the use of nuclear weapons against non-nuclear weapon states would also be an important step (Singh 2005).

> India has long held the view that the total elimination of nuclear weapons is the only absolute guarantee against the use or threat of use of nuclear weapons....The non-aligned States consider such assurances a matter of urgent attention....The NAM Coordinating Bureau called for the conclusion, at the Conference on Disarmament, of a universal, unconditional and legally binding instrument on security assurances as a matter or priority, pending the total elimination of nuclear weapons.

While considering the issue of effective international arrangements for assuring non-nuclear weapon State against the use or threat of use of nuclear weapons, the Conference must also consider the related and complementary proposals on reaching an understanding on no-first use of nuclear weapons and negotiating a Convention prohibiting the use of nuclear weapons in any circumstances. Besides its other benefits, such as rendering nuclear weapons redundant and reducing their salience for military strategy, such a Convention will reinforce security assurances (Prasad 2006c).

As noted below, negative security assurances are particularly linked to nuclear weapon-free zones, but there is resistance to allowing states like India, Israel, and Pakistan to sign the relevant protocols to NWFZ agreements by NNWS because of the implied recognition of these three non-NPT signatories as NWS within the context of the NPT (Chaffee and Wurst 2002). Unilateral NSA declarations by any of them might be the way to avoid that implication.

Once again, it is possible to see India's explicit support for legally binding NSA as a risk-free commitment, on the assumption that a commitment equal to what the NWS are likely to make will be acceptable. In the meantime India's commitments fall short of commitments made by NWS in 1995 and 2000. Remember, the question we are asking here is not whether India's commitments are up to the standards of NWS *behaviour*. We are trying to assess whether India is to become a DNWS that mimics the unacceptable records of the NWS, thereby simply adding to the problem of states with nuclear weapons that avoid their responsibilities, or whether India as a DNWS will offer a superior model and act as a potential spur to improved NWS behaviour.

Reduced operational status

Reducing the operational status of nuclear weapons, agreed to by NWS in the 13 practical steps of the 2000 RevCon (Part I, para 15.9), refers primarily to extending launch procedures to ensure against unauthorized launches, or authorized launches in response to false warnings of attack. Such de-alerting ultimately involves removing warheads from delivery vehicles, but it can also be aided by policy and doctrinal changes. One such policy is to forgo launch-on-warning postures with a policy commitment to refuse, even if technically possible, to launch a counterattack based only on warning of an attack—deciding instead to withhold counterattack at least until an incoming attack can be confirmed by a detected detonation. A doctrinal restraint on retaliation is also provided through no-first-use commitments.

NWS have collectively made formal commitments only with regard to de-alerting, but Indian policies and posture engage all three issues: de-alerting, no-launch-on-warning, and no-first-use.

RAND's 2001 study reports that

> India's objective is to create...a "force-in-being." This term refers to a nuclear deterrent that consists of available, but dispersed, components: unassembled nuclear warheads, with their components stored separately under strict civilian control, and dedicated delivery systems kept either in storage or in readiness away from their operational areas—all of which can be brought together as rapidly as required to create a usable deterrent force during a supreme emergency (Tellis 2001).

The forces-in-being posture is said to rely on a capacity to retaliate "within a matter of hours to weeks"—clearly a reduced operational status. India in turn urges de-alerting on the NWS: "The nuclear weapon States should also take practical steps to lower the alert status, through gradual de-alerting actions of their strategic weapons, consistent with the defensive role of nuclear weapons" (Singh 2005).

India is said to be pursuing the capacity for retaliation that is delayed but assured (no launch-on-warning). Tellis (2001) writes:

> Because Indian security managers feel confident that the possibility of nuclear weapons use in South Asia is remote, they believe that their ability to retaliate with certainty is more important than their ability to retaliate with speed. As India's strategic capabilities evolve, however, New Delhi will be able to retaliate with both certainty and speed.

India formally espouses a no-first-use doctrine. The Natural Resources Defense Council reports:

> During 2001, including during heightened tension with Pakistan, Indian government officials have reaffirmed India's commitment to a no-first-use policy for nuclear weapons. An Indian foreign ministry official told *Defense News* in 2002, however, that a "'no first strike' policy does not mean India will not have a first strike capability." He explained that India was "working toward having a first strike capability," but that it was a political decision how to exercise this option within the "no first strike" policy (Natural Resources Defense Council 2002).

The no-first-use policy, however, is not consistent with the CCS insistence on the prerogative to use nuclear weapons in response to attacks with biological or chemical weapons.

Diminishing Role for Nuclear Weapons

The 2000 RevCon final statement agreed that one of the steps "leading to nuclear disarmament" to be taken by NWS is to ensure "a diminishing role for nuclear weapons in security policies to minimize the risk that these weapons will ever be used and to facilitate the process of their total elimination" (Part I, para 15.9).

It is obvious that India is in the process of dramatically increasing the role of nuclear weapons in its security policies. Furthermore, the US decision to fully accept India's nuclear weapons development and posture is bound to have the impact of inflating the political value of nuclear weapons to India. Nevertheless, India has publicly supported the reduction of the strategic significance of nuclear weapons:

> [T]he nuclear weapon States should take visible steps to reduce the salience of nuclear weapons in their strategic calculus. Since nuclear weapons are not really usable, efforts should be directed at taking steps, in the first instance, towards reducing their importance in security approaches. India believes in this approach and has therefore followed a policy of "No First Use." A step in this direction would be a global No-First-Use agreement. An agreement by Nuclear Weapon States ruling out the use of nuclear weapons against non-nuclear weapon states would also be an important step (Singh 2005).

India declares its readiness "to multilateralise our no-first-use commitment so as to reduce the salience of nuclear weapons in the strategic realm" (Prasad 2006a), but given the ambiguity of its own no-first-use declaration and the resistance of NWS to the proposition, it is a readiness unlikely to be tested any time soon.

Nuclear Weapon Free Zones

The 1995 RevCon noted that "the co-operation of all the nuclear-weapon States and their respect and support for the relevant protocols is necessary for the maximum effectiveness of such nuclear weapon free zones (NWFZ) and the relevant protocols" (Decision 2, para 7). The standard, as noted above, for negative security assurance statements linked to NWFZ is for the relevant protocols to be confined to NPT signatories; in other words, acknowledged NWS (Spector and Ohide 2005).

At the 1999 meeting of the ASEAN foreign ministers, a meeting of the commission of the Treaty of Bangkok (OPANAL 1995) was convened and plans were made to develop a protocol for NSA. India reportedly indicated a willingness to sign the protocol. However, Article 3 of the protocol explicitly states it will "be open for signature by the People's Republic of China, the French Republic, the Russian Federation, the United Kingdom of Great Britain and Northern Ireland and the US of America."

While civilian nuclear co-operation effectively treats India as a nuclear weapon state, a *de facto* nuclear weapon state is still not the same as a NWS. Thus it is likely that the only way that India could meet its NWS-equivalent responsibility with regard to NSA is through unilateral declarations.

Safeguarding Surplus NWS Fissile Materials

It is the objective of the NPT and IAEA safeguards system to gradually and eventually bring all fissile material under safeguarded controls and so render them unavailable for use in nuclear weapons. As part of this system, NWS are encouraged to identify materials that were originally developed for weapons purposes but are now surplus and to bring them under safeguards. As the NWS meet their Article VI obligations, those surpluses will increase and progressively more material will come under safeguards. At the 1995 RevCon, NWS agreed to the importance of such measures:

> Nuclear fissile material transferred from military use to peaceful nuclear activities should, as soon as practicable, be placed under Agency safeguards in the framework of the voluntary safeguards agreement in place with the nuclear-weapon States. Safeguards should be universally applied once the complete elimination of nuclear weapons has been achieved (Decision 2, para 13).

The US-India deal provides for certain Indian facilities to be designated exclusively civilian and thus brought under IAEA safeguards. Calling for a "credible plan", the agreement allows India to retain the prerogative to decide on the separation of civilian and military nuclear facilities and programs. India is then required to file a declaration regarding its civil facilities with the IAEA and to conclude "all legal steps" for IAEA safeguards agreements, with the added provision that the safeguards on civilian facilities are to remain in place in perpetuity. The US legislation does not require India's adherence to the additional protocol, but does require "substantial progress" toward that end (Squassoni and Parillo 2006). India promised in the July 18, 2005 agreement to sign and adhere to the additional protocol, but, as is the case with NWS, the protocol would apply only to those facilities that India has defined as civilian. Obviously, at this point India is unlikely to declare any fissile materials produced for military purposes to be surplus to its military requirements.

Trade and Assistance

Article I of the NPT prohibits NWS from "in any way" assisting, encouraging, or inducing any NNWS to acquire nuclear weapons.

A recent report of the US Congressional Research Service (Squassoni 2006) examines India's history of nuclear co-operation with Iran and generally finds that, while India does not necessarily share Washington's approach to Iran, it nevertheless has consistently opposed any Iranian pursuit of a nuclear weapons capability, while offering modest help to Iran in its effort to develop nuclear energy.

The US legislation calls on India to work with the US to prevent the spread of enrichment and reprocessing facilities "to any state that does not already possess full-scale, functioning enrichment and reprocessing plants" and to support international efforts toward that end. The legislation also calls on India to enact and enforce export control laws to harmonize its laws, regulations, and practices with the requirements of the MTCR and the NSG (Squassoni and Parillo 2006).

When the original deal was announced, India essentially agreed to accept these "responsibilities and practices," including "refraining from transfer of enrichment and reprocessing technologies to states that do not have them and supporting international efforts to limit their spread" (White House 2005).

This provision has been US policy for some time, and in 2004 the US tried to persuade the NSG to adopt the same policy. However, NSG states, operating on consensus, did not agree. The provision thus is not part of any NPT, IAEA, or NSG obligation. In general, India claims to maintain strict export control policies and practices consistent with the NPT and other international obligations:

> India may not be a party to the NPT, but, our conduct has always been consistent with the key provisions of the Treaty as they apply to nuclear weapon States. Article I of the NPT obliges a nuclear weapon state not to transfer nuclear weapons to any other country or to assist any other country to acquire

> them. India's record in this regard is impeccable and a matter
> of public knowledge....

> ...Article III requires a party to the Treaty to provide nuclear
> materials and related equipment to any other country only
> under safeguards. India's policies of international co-operation
> in the nuclear field have always conformed to this principle....

> ...We are committed to further strengthening our regulatory
> framework in this regard in keeping with changing technical
> and security challenges. India has never been and will never be
> a source of proliferation. This has been reiterated at the
> highest political levels and is an article of faith of our foreign
> policy (Singh 2005).

India has reported on its progress in implementing UN Security Council
Resolution 1540 with regard to transfer regulations, preventing the
diversion of materials to non-state actors, and supporting missile non-
proliferation (United Nations 2004).

Reporting

Transparency on the part of NWS is a growing demand of the NNWS
states party to the NPT. At the 2000 RevCon, NWS agreed to greater
transparency and accountability through the reporting provision agreed to
as one of the thirteen practical steps toward disarmament:

> Regular reports, within the framework of the strengthened
> review process for the Non-Proliferation Treaty, by all States'
> parties on the implementation of article VI and paragraph 4(c)
> of the 1995 Decision on "Principles and Objectives from
> Nuclear Non-Proliferation and Disarmament," and recalling
> the advisory opinion of the International Court of Justice of 8
> July 1996 (Part I, para 15.12).

In addition, states agreed in general to increased transparency regarding
nuclear capabilities (Part I, para 15.9).

It is clear that, as an emerging nuclear state, India will not easily adopt
transparency. Estimates of its current and intended arsenal vary. Tellis
(2001) puts its intended arsenal at about 150 warheads. The number and
types of delivery vehicles are unclear, although speculation includes
aircraft, ground mobile, and sea-based systems (Tellis 2001).

President Bush says that the US-India deal will "bring India into the
international nuclear nonproliferation mainstream and will increase the

transparency of India's entire civilian nuclear program" (Klug 2006), but under the NPT there are also transparency requirements regarding the military programs and arsenals. To the extent that India has declared itself on the matter of transparency, the emphasis has been rather heavily on cautions related to what it regards as security requirements.

> Measures to enhance transparency in armaments must, therefore, be based on full respect for these rights (of self defence and to acquire arms for security). Also they should take into account the legitimate security needs of States and the principle of undiminished security at the lowest possible level of armaments.

> The measures to promote transparency in armaments at the regional and sub-regional levels should take into account the specific characteristics of the region and strive to enhance the security of States and build confidence among them. Transparency also presupposes a modicum of peaceful intentions and stability; otherwise it may only reveal vulnerability.

> As with other confidence-building measures, measures to promote transparency in armaments should be voluntary and mutually agreed upon by all States; only then would they be able to secure the widest possible participation and effectively contribute to the process of confidence-building (Prasad 2006d).

Conclusion

In summary, India can be said to be meeting, or willing to meet, NWS standards in terms of declared commitments with regard to reduced operational status of weapons systems, NWFZ, and trade and assistance regulations. India has accepted the obligation to disarm, although it is not party to any legally binding agreement to that end. On the CTBT, FMCT, NSA, a diminished role for nuclear weapons, safeguarding surplus materials, and reporting, India's declared commitments fall short of the formal commitments and obligations (as distinct from behaviour) of NWS.

India's rhetorical commitment to total nuclear disarmament is unambiguous. Support for disarmament within a specified time frame distinguishes India's stand from the postures of the NWS. At the same time, its prominent insistence that disarmament must be "non-discriminatory" and pursued "on the basis of equality" links India's commitment directly to the behaviour of NWS—a fairly reliable assurance that its rhetoric is not about to be put to the test. Unlike the NWS, India is not under a legal obligation to disarm, although its declared commitment to disarmament reflects its recognition of the global norm against any long-term retention of nuclear weapons.

India's unilateral moratorium on nuclear testing was made a bilateral commitment in the July 2005 joint statement, with US legislation making it clear that the agreement would end in the event of further testing. India continues to reject the CTBT, but implies that in "a positive environment" it would sign on, suggesting that ratification of the CTBT would be a reasonable condition for support for the deal in the NSG.

India supports negotiations toward an FMCT but refuses to join a moratorium on the production of fissile materials for weapons purposes. US legislation includes a (non-binding) policy statement to pursue a moratorium on Indian production of fissile materials for weapons purposes, but links it to a similar moratorium in Pakistan and India. Given the NWS moratorium and India's insistence on being treated on an equal basis, it would be reasonable to insist that an Indian exemption to NSG guidelines be contingent on India's joining that moratorium.

India currently stands by a qualified, unilateral NSA declaration, and supports legally binding NSA. Its NSA declaration is qualified because it reserves the right to respond to chemical or biological threats/attacks with a nuclear threat/attack; thus its commitment falls short of the 1995 and 2000 commitments made by the NWS.

Indian nuclear forces appear to be on a substantially reduced readiness status, meaning that India is essentially in full compliance with the NWS commitment.

It would be hard to argue that India is on a trajectory of diminishing importance of nuclear weapons in its national security calculus. Even so, in comparison with most other NWS, India's minimum deterrence doctrine can be seen as an intention to limit the role of nuclear weapons in its security arrangements.

India is supportive of NWFZ and has expressed its willingness to sign protocols giving such zones security assurances against threats from NWS. However, inasmuch as that would implicitly recognize India as a NWS, any security assurances given by India to NWFZ will have to come through unilateral declarations.

India does not regard itself to be in a position to declare any fissile materials for weapons purposes surplus to its military needs. By placing more of its civilian facilities, though not all, under IAEA inspections it could perhaps make a modest claim in this direction, but as long as production of fissile materials for weapons purposes continues it cannot be regarded as being in compliance.

India appears to be in full compliance with the obligations of NWS in Article I of the NPT, adheres to MTCR and NSG guidelines, and has reported on its compliance with Resolution 1540. In the 2005 joint statement with the US, India goes further and agrees with the US not to transfer enrichment and reprocessing technologies to states that do not already have them.

India is highly wary of transparency in matters related to its nuclear arsenal. Transparency in civilian programs is a declared objective of the US-India deal, but India links transparency in military nuclear programs to agreement on transparency measures with "all States."

Nuclear Bullying: India-US Nuclear Relations

David Mutimer

From the moment of the first atomic explosion over Hiroshima, nuclear weapons capability has been central to our world order. The relationship between the capacity to use nuclear arms and leadership in the international community was evident as the two superpowers were also the first nuclear powers, and the relationship was then cemented by the consonance of the club of those legally nuclear-armed with those holding permanent seats on the UN Security Council. The decision by India in 1998 not only to test nuclear explosives but to announce them as weapons tests therefore poses a particular challenge to the received world order. As we in general, and Canadians in particular, turn to think about how to organize our relations with a nuclear-armed India, it is important to keep questions of world order in mind.

I use the term world order advisedly in this context. The consonance of legal nuclear possession with membership in the P-5 is often considered as a simple expression of power: the largest, most powerful states in the international system have both the most powerful weapons and the seats at the most powerful tables. However, this simple relationship is clearly no longer true, and it probably never was—certainly not while Taiwan held the China seat on the Security Council. More importantly, both world order and leadership are social terms, pointing to the way that power considerations are embedded within social relations even at the global level. Such an assertion is not novel, and should not by this point be surprising. However, while there has been considerable attention given to the social nature of world politics, little of it has been directed at questions of nuclear weapons or, ironically, at the place and nature of power.

This paper aims to assist in redressing these lacunae by considering the history of US-Indian relations on nuclear weapons in terms of a metaphor of "bullying." Bullying, of course, is a common metaphor in the popular, and even scholarly, discourse on international relations. Our received notions about the practices of international life stress the direct application of coercive force in a fashion immediately reminiscent of the stereotypical view of bullying. In the memories of most of our childhoods there are instances, greater or fewer in number depending on our good fortune, of suffering at the hands of bullies. Usually, these bullies are children physically larger than ourselves, either because they are older or because they have grown at a faster rate. The bully uses this advantage in size to get his or her way, to force or cow us to fall into whatever line he or she has chosen. This unpleasant, and all-too-common, experience serves as a ready metaphor for the interaction of states in a system in which power is distributed unevenly, and in which the direct application of physical force seems to hold a pride of place.

As is rather too usual in the discipline of international relations, however, we have taken an idea too easily, without exploring any of the baggage that comes with that idea. We have, in other words, accepted the common and superficial understanding of a term without considering the expert views of those who study the phenomenon in its own right. What I hope to show is that even a cursory examination of the literature on bullying reveals a complex social understanding of the practice, and it is a complexity that can provide theoretical insight into international social practice. I begin, therefore, with an attempt to deepen the bullying metaphor by drawing on the psychological literature to illuminate interstate relations in terms of the relations among bully, victim, and peers. Using that more complex metaphor as my frame, I then provide an account of US-Indian relations as the relations between bully and victim, in order to suggest ways the metaphor can help us understand the social dynamic of these relations and draw conclusions about the way forward in the relationship.

Bullying States

A leading student of bullying, Dan Olweus, defines it as follows: "A person is being bullied when he or she is exposed, repeatedly and over time, to [deliberate] negative actions on the part of one or more other persons" (Olweus 1991). Olweus proceeds to qualify this simple definition in a number of ways that are useful for my purposes. The first is that bullying takes place between people of unequal power: "There should be a certain imbalance in the strength relations (an asymmetric power relationship): The person who is exposed to the negative actions has difficulty defending him/herself and is somewhat helpless against the person or persons who harass" (Olweus 1991). This qualification accords with our expectations about bullying, but is still important to keep in mind.

Olweus' second qualification concerns the phrase he stresses: "repeatedly and over time'. Bullying is a social relationship, it is not a single incident."[1] The ongoing, social nature of bullying is also common to our general understanding of the term, but is not a feature of the metaphor that has translated well to international relations, in which the relations among states are so often treated asocially. The social nature of bullying, however, is crucial to deepening its metaphorical uses. Olweus continues to draw a distinction "between direct bullying—with relatively open attacks on the victim—and indirect bullying in the form of social isolation and exclusion from a group" (Olweus 1991). As we shall see below, social exclusion is an important feature of the bullying metaphor as applied to the relationship between India and the US, and is a feature of social life not generally considered in international relations. In some more recent work, Debra Peplar and her collaborators have found that peer group involvement, particularly their involvement as an "audience" for bullying episodes, is an important feature of the bullying relationship (Peplar, Craig, and O'Connell 1999).

The social features of bullying, captured in the role of peers and in the distinction between direct and indirect bullying, make the metaphor particularly appealing for application to international relations. The bullying metaphor provides a way of thinking about power that captures both relational and structural power, and does so in a way that allows for thinking about state interactions as social relationships.[2]

In particular, thinking about interstate relations as bullying relations suggests that we can see iterated instances of the expression of relational power forming a structural relation of dominance between two states, a relation that is embedded within, supported, and reproduced by a society of "peers." In the case of children's bullying, what we tend to see is brief, individual instances of aggressive behaviour from the "bully" to the "victim." What the social features of the relationship, stressed by Olweus and Peplar, mean is that "bullying" is really about the ongoing relationship between bully and victim that is produced and reproduced by these moments of violence, but then fostered and sustained by the expectations

---

[1] Actually, Olweus allows for a particularly serious single incident to count as bullying "'under certain circumstances', but stresses that in general bullying is a pattern of 'negative actions.'"

[2] The distinction between relational and structural power was introduced widely in the International relations discourse by Susan Strange in her *States and Markets* (London: Pinter, 1988). For an attempt to use the division and move beyond it to a more sophisticated understanding of power, see Keith Krause, "Military Statecraft: Power and Influence in Soviet and American Arms Transfer Relationships," *International Studies Quarterly*, 35 (3), 1991.

of all those in the social group: bullies, victims, and peers. In international relations, we have a great deal of difficulty thinking about stable patterns of social relations that are not clearly institutionalized, particularly patterns of social hierarchy, and we have notorious difficulty thinking about power.[3]

In order to deepen the bullying metaphor still further and to develop a more rounded account of bullying, I have identified a series of key elements of the bullying relationship to use to illuminate the US-Indian case below. This series of key elements is summarized in Table I below, in which I expand on each of these key features including the central ones I have just introduced.

	Children	States
Direct bullying	Physical aggression, sometimes using weapons Verbal taunting	Physical aggression, always using weapons (border clashes, gunboat diplomacy) Verbal aggression (from the demarche to the outright verbal assault)
Indirect bullying	Using others to attack the victim Using the social structure to harm the victim "Social isolation and exclusion from the group"	Proxy wars, arming enemies (Pakistan-US relations) Using IGOs to harm (IMF, World Bank, supplier control groups) India's non-alignment, its not being welcomed into the Security Council, its not being asked to join the supplier groups, etc.
Peer reinforcement	Attention and joint involvement Group coherence	Expressions of support, joining in (NATO in Kosovo) Group coherence seen in (NATO in Kosovo)

---

[3] These deficits in the international relations literature are being redressed in the various forms of literature that take as their premise the social constitution of international life. For an important recent statement of the most mainstream of these positions, but one which starts from iterated social interactions, see Alexander Wendt, Social Theory of International Politics (Cambridge: Cambridge UP, 1999).

Peer behaviour modelling	Acting in the same way toward the victim	Not sure if this is evidenced in states interactions, although analogies could easily be found
Attitude to the bully	Respect, friendship	Acceptance of the dominance of the bully (recognition of US leadership around the world—even by those who contest it)
Attitude to the victim	Less respect, friendship than to the bully	Lack of respect has been a constant theme of India's diplomacy
Adult intervention	Crucial, if seen too infrequently. Subject of much of the policy recommendation	Impossible. The key to anarchic society is that there are no "adult" analogies. This is a major, crucial difference
Nature of change	Anecdotal evidence that "standing up" to the bully alters the relationship	If we think of Indian testing as a response to extended bullying, it seems to have increased the respect accorded the victim

Table 1: Key features of the bullying metaphor

Direct versus Indirect Bullying

The first key feature is the nature of the bullying episodes, and in particular the distinction researchers draw between direct and indirect bullying. Direct bullying involves relatively open attacks on the victim by the bully. These can take the form of physical violence or verbal assaults (Olweus 1991). These kinds of incidents are relatively easy to see in international relations: small-scale military assaults and gun-boat diplomacy, punitive economic sanctions, and the so-called public diplomacy of denunciation. Indeed, it is the ease with which apparent incidents of direct bullying are seen between states that has made for the ready application of the term to international events.

For my purposes in this work, indirect bullying is the more interesting. As I noted above, Olweus describes this as "social isolation and exclusion from the group," and in some of her work Peplar speaks of getting others to attack the victim and using social structure to harm the victim without becoming directly involved. Here the analogies in international life are also numerous and also important: in the case of using others to do your work for you, the Cold War was full of proxy violence as a means of applying pressure and escaping responsibility. In the case of India, the US has been arming Pakistan for decades. Instances of the use of indirect harm through structure are also legion. The US in particular consistently uses its capacity to influence international organizations to harm other states: very overtly in the case of the Organization of American States and Cuba; for example, less overtly in places like the G-8, the IMF and World Bank.

Role of Peers

The place of peers in the study of bullying is particularly revealing when we make use of the metaphor in international relations. The common expectation of bullying is that it is an isolated phenomenon—both that it is not very common, and that it is almost entirely a dyadic relationship between the bully (or small group of bullies) and the victim (or small group of victims). However, research on children's bullying has tended to contradict these assumptions: bullying is widespread, and peer involvement is crucial in the ongoing social relations that are produced. There are three key features of peer involvement for understanding the bullying relationship: peer reinforcement, attitudes to the bully, and attitudes to the victim (Peplar, Craig, and O'Connell 1999).

The first point is that the attitudes and behaviour of the peer group tend to reinforce bullying behaviour, "locking it into place." Peers pay attention to bullying behaviour, often approvingly, and may even become involved on the side of the bully. What is particularly interesting is that peer group coherence can be established through such intervention. In other words, not only is the bullying relationship not simply a dyadic relation between bully and victim, but the violence can serve a social function in developing a collective identity. Again, there are important analogies in international life. Episodes of international violence do not take place in social isolation; rather, they receive expressions either of support or condemnation. Often, others will become involved or directly or indirectly—supplying troops, supplies, or diplomatic support. Recall, for example, the way in which "the West" almost reflexively supported British military action in the Falklands/Malvinas conflict, despite the ease with which it could have been constructed as one of the last anti-colonial wars. Even the US, with its strong ties to Latin America and in the face of the Monroe Doctrine, did not oppose British action.

Perhaps even more interesting than the simple act of support is the way in which collaborative violence can forge group coherence internationally.[4] In the instance of NATO's war in Kosovo, NATO in-group coherence was at least as important as the humanitarian motivations for the attacks. NATO was grasping for internal meaning. Ten years after the end of the Cold War, it still was not clear what NATO's role could be in a new Europe. Acting as the effective military arm of the United Nations in areas such as Yugoslavia within its geographic competence seemed to provide a ready-made solution to the identity crisis of the alliance. So important was it to NATO to establish this role that the member states did not even consider it necessary to be mandated by the United Nations before acting as its agent. I am not necessarily making the argument that the Kosovo bombing was the act of a bully (although it is an obvious case with which to further explore the utility of the metaphor), but I would note that bullies rarely attack those they consider physically capable of inflicting harm on them.

The second key feature of the role of peers in episodes of bullying is the attitudes that develop toward the bully on the part of the peers. The bullying research suggests that peers tend to develop a greater respect for bullies, and to show greater friendship toward the bully than the victim. Again, this appears to be a promising way to think about international relations, and is, in fact, one of my principal reasons for exploring the metaphor. Ideas of prestige and social leadership are largely foreign to our discipline, and we tend to equate leadership with simple dominance.[5] The bullying analogy suggests instead that dominance provides the means for repeated actions that in turn generate prestige, which is accorded to the "bully" by other states. For example, while outwardly deploring repeated acts of violence by the US, USSR, and the PRC during the Cold War, all the states in the system continued to accord them the "respect" due leaders. Importantly, this was not only those states in their own "sphere," where leadership might have been generated by a more direct application of dominance. More formally, there is also a body of International Relations literature that suggests that states tend toward "bandwagoning"

---

[4] There has been some literature that explores this phenomenon in international relations. See, in particular, Bradley Klein, *Strategic Studies and World Order* (Cambridge: Cambridge University Press, 1994). In a similar vein, David Campbell's work has examined the way in which security threats can forge a domestic collective identity in his *Writing Security: US foreign policy and the politics of identity* (Minneapolis: University of Minnesota Press, 1992).

[5] A notable exception in this regard is the work of Jennifer Milliken, who has taken issues of prestige among states very seriously.

behaviour rather than balancing threatening states—although the latter does happen as well.[6]

Finally, the attitudes toward the victim tend to replicate those of the bully, seeing the victim as weak and deserving of abuse. This observation suggests a question that may well be worth asking: Do states tend to "follow-the-leader" in aggressive, dominating behaviour toward weaker states? I will suggest below that in the case of India and nuclear weapons, the answer seems to be yes for states as well as for schoolchildren.

Nature of Change

A crucial feature of any developed bullying metaphor is an exploration of the way in which the relationship changes. In the literature on bullying among children, the means of generating change is of central concern. Those who study bullying among children do so in order to prevent it and to stop it when it occurs. While students of international relations may not have quite the same normative drive to stop bullying by states, clearly the means of changing that relationship will be important both normatively and analytically. Unless we are willing to argue that behaviour analogous to bullying is quite acceptable among states, there is some normative presumption to work for its change. However, even ignoring its normative importance, the issue of change is analytically relevant. States subjected to bullying will seek to overcome the bullying relationship, and so, as students, we will want to understand the actions the victims take. The problem with generating analogies from the literature on children is that work on change focuses on authoritative, third party intervention, particularly intervention by teachers and parents.

Bullying among children takes place in a context of a clear set of legitimate governing arrangements, subordinating children to the governance of adults. Thus change focuses on the ways in which adults can intervene to break the patterns of bullying and to prevent them from beginning. International relations, simply put, does not work this way. Indeed, the closest analogy would be that the schoolyard relationship is the realm of the domestic, or municipal. Formal hierarchical governance characterizes law and politics within states, not between them. This is true, however far down the road of international norms and rules you wish to travel from the Realist extreme. Even if international relations is entirely governed by normative conventions and intersubjectively constituted rules of communal governance, those norms and rules

---

[6] For a discussion of bandwagoning behaviour and its alternatives, as well as a useful review of the wider discussion in international relations, see Stephen Walt, *The Origin of Alliances* (Ithaca: Cornell, 1988).

produce a horizontally rather than vertically organized form of governance.

The difference between children's bullying in the context of a clearly hierarchical order and among states in anarchy places very clear limits on the applicability of the analogy I am developing—international relations is more like the island in *Lord of the Flies* than the schoolyards of bullying research.[7] Nevertheless, I believe the metaphor is still worth exploring, precisely in this context, because thinking of bullying as an ongoing social relationship reveals patterns of hierarchy that do not conform to the formal patterns of institutional governance. Such patterns of hierarchy are apparent in studying the relations among states, where we see plenty of evidence of hierarchy, but not the formal hierarchy of domestic government.

The second point about change is also centrally important to thinking about bullying relations among states: What happens when the victims become sick and tired of the bullying and seek to redress the problem themselves, without authoritative intervention? An answer to this question may provide insight into patterns of social behaviour among states that do not have recourse to parental analogies. By way of a preliminary answer to this question, I will tell a short family story. My father was, apparently, the victim of bullying by a larger child at school. My father also has a truly remarkable temper—a trait I am sorry to say I have inherited. As he tells the story, one day when the bully pushed him too far, he "snapped" and when he realized what was happening, he was halfway across a rugby pitch, dragging the other child by the hair. Needless to say, this realization startled him somewhat, as here he was with a bigger, stronger boy, a boy who had been quite willing to be violent, and my father's actions were likely to provoke even further displeasure from this lad! He decided that safety lay in continuing, and so crossed the field before letting him go. The bully, apparently, never bothered him again.

This story suggests that standing up to a bully can result in a profound change in the social relationship between bully, victim, and peers. Certainly, as I shall argue below, in the case of the US and India, this observation seems borne out.

---

[7] In this context, it is important to recognise that the children in *Lord of the Flies* were thoroughly socialized in a hierarchical governing arrangement, which was then removed by the fact of the accident. While states were never so socialised and removed, international society cannot be disconnected from the societies it surrounds and that surround it.

Problems and Limitations

As I have just noted, there is at least one considerable problem with the bullying metaphor, insofar as interstate relations do not take place within a set of authoritative and hierarchical governing arrangements. There are several other problems that I want to acknowledge before using the metaphor to consider the case of India and the US. The first problem is that states are not children—yet they are also not adults. Humans pass through a sequence of developmental stages; states do not. They do not grow up. While it is true that states are socialized in various ways, they do not respond to biological or social pressures to "mature" in particular ways. Attempts to treat human collectives as if they were developing human beings have proven to be, at the very least, ill-conceived and at worst positively damaging. Consider, for example, the not inconsiderable damage done in the Third World by the ideas of the "modernization" school, which sought to lead "immature" states through the "developmental" stages of modernization. Such damage is not limited ideologically: consider the comparable damage done by those keen on moving peoples through the different "stages" which lead to a communist utopia.

The second problem is that there are affective associations of bullying. The idea of bullying horrifies adults. By and large, we identify with the victims, and assume that the bullies are dysfunctional. In fact, the implicit assumption from which bullying research begins is that bullying is the behaviour of socially dysfunctional, aggressive children. Notice that Olweus, in the definition I used to begin this discussion, defines the actions constitutive of bullying as "negative." These affective associations pose problems at the international level. For example, when I have mentioned the idea to colleagues of developing bullying as a metaphor to think about India and the US, I have generally had two responses: "Which one is the bully?" and "Oh, poor little India." Both of these were said with tongue in cheek, the latter dripping with sarcasm.

This last problem is particularly tricky. I do not want to argue that if there are social processes analogous to bullying among states, they are necessarily to be judged in the same way as we judge bullying among children. Consider again the example I raised above of NATO and the bombing of Yugoslavia. The social processes surrounding the bombing seem analogous to those surrounding episodes of bullying, in interesting ways. In particular, if we think of the US and Yugoslavia (or Serbia) in the roles of bully and victim, the behaviour of the NATO in-group seems revealingly analogous to the observed behaviour of child peers in episodes of bullying. However, regardless of our attitudes to the Kosovo bombing,

I expect there are few who would identify with Yugoslavia/Serbia/ Milosevic as one would with a child being bullied in school.[8] Thus, the labels *bully* and *victim* may be the wrong ones, for affective rather than analytic reasons. If, as I hope to show below, it makes some sense to think about the US as a bully and India as a victim in the case of their relations on nuclear issues, this should not *automatically* be read as saying that the US is behaving "badly" or "dysfunctionally," nor that the Indians deserve our sympathy. Rather, I am trying to see whether similar patterns of social behaviour are produced among states, whether we can use that to understand instances of conflict, and ultimately whether we can generate means of conflict prevention and/or management.

"Poor Little India"

Making use of these key features of the bully metaphor, I will now provide an analytic account of US-Indian relations over the question of nuclear weapons, revolving around the Indian test of 1998. I divide this account chronologically into five periods: from the test of fusion weapons to the Indian nuclear test of 1974; from 1974 to the Gulf War of 1991; from the Gulf War to September 1996; from September 1996 to May 1998; and then from May 1998 to the present. Following this account, I will suggest the sorts of questions that the metaphor raises, and why I think they may be questions worth answering.

Throughout the first period, beginning with the US test of a hydrogen bomb, India worked consistently for a nuclear test ban treaty and for nuclear disarmament. Initially, the treatment of India by the US was only mildly dismissive and exclusionary. The US refused to negotiate nuclear disarmament, and what discussions there were on a nuclear test ban were conducted bilaterally with the Soviet Union, or between the two superpowers along with the minor involvement of the UK. The first major problem in the US-Indian nuclear relationship arose over the NPT. Here India was subjected to an important exclusion, largely on the part of the US, but with support from its "peers." The NPT was signed in 1968 and entered into force in 1970. It required all states that had not tested nuclear weapons by 1968 to renounce them, but it did not require those that had tested to give them up.

---

[8] In order to be as open as possible, I supported the NATO intervention in Kosovo, but not the particular means chosen. Intervention to prevent genocide—even if that were not the sole motivation, is surely to be applauded. However, the reliance on bombing served to exacerbate the very problem it was purportedly designed to prevent. It did, however, save countless NATO lives.

The NPT agreement left India decidedly on the outside. China had tested its nuclear weapons by 1968, and so was recognized to be a NWS; India had not, so if it was to join the NPT, it would have to do it by renouncing its nuclear capability. This last is an important point to emphasize. The treaty does not have provision for admitting states that tested nuclear weapons after 1968 as NWS, on a par with the US, the Soviet Union (now Russia), the UK, France, and China. To do so would require an amendment of the treaty. This means that India is barred from participating in the global non-proliferation regime, except on terms set by others and that it explicitly rejects. Thus, the NPT was a fairly direct slap in the face for India. India was known to have a nuclear program, and to be reasonably close to developing a nuclear explosive, while the NPT was under negotiation. The line drawn in the NPT was set in such a way as to admit China, which had only just made it. It is notable that China bordered India and did not have the finest of relations with India! The Indian position in these discussions, which was that they would agree to renounce nuclear weapons in return, not for non-proliferation, but for nuclear disarmament, was ignored.

In terms of its international prestige, the result of the NPT negotiation was deeply offensive to the Indians. India sees itself as state comparable to China: its population is second in the world only to China's and it has an ancient civilization as old and distinguished as the Chinese. And yet it is never treated internationally with the same respect accorded to the Chinese state, but is rhetorically linked to Pakistan, a state a fraction of its size and without either the ancient heritage or the modern tradition of democratic governance. Quite reasonably, India expects to be treated as China is treated. And yet China is accorded a permanent seat on the UN Security Council, and the NPT enshrines China's right to a legal nuclear arsenal, while denying the same to India on the arbitrary basis of a few short years' lag in testing.

As a result, in 1974, India completed its nuclear program and tested its first nuclear device. It was, however, a weak attempt to stand up to the nuclear states, as India did not announce that this was a nuclear *weapons* test, but rather a peaceful nuclear explosive, and announced it had no plans to build weapons.[9] The consequences of the test were further ostracism by the US and its peers, and even more extensive instances of

---

[9] Quite remarkably, the NPT allowed for the peaceful uses of nuclear explosives, and even imposed an obligation on nuclear weapon states to make nuclear explosives available to non-nuclear weapon states for peaceful purposes. At the time the NPT was signed, for example, it was considered that large earth-moving projects could be facilitated with the judicious application of a little atomic might!

"bullying." The US led in the creation of a series of "supplier control groups," which regulated access to weapons and related technologies. The first of these were groups designed to control the spread of nuclear technology, and were created in direct response to India's explosion. They were followed by controls on chemical, biological, and missile technology. India was not invited to participate in any of these groups, despite the fact that the test demonstrated technological capacity in nuclear explosives, and India later developed an indigenous ballistic missile program. The US also supplied arms and military assistance to Pakistan throughout the period from the test to the Gulf War of 1991. These arms were used, among other things, to do battle with India on a number of occasions.

Throughout this period following its first nuclear test, India continued to seek a comprehensive test ban treaty and negotiations on nuclear disarmament. Here the pattern remained the same as it had in the first period: the US refused to negotiate disarmament, barely negotiated on a test ban, but continued to insist that India renounce its nuclear program and join the NPT as a NNWS.

The end of the Cold War and the Gulf War of 1991 altered the circumstances of the US-India nuclear relationship, and ushered in a third distinct period. These two events changed the way that arms in general and nuclear arms in particular were thought about in "the West." Briefly, central to this change was that the idea of "non-proliferation" came to be applied to all forms of weapons technology, not just to nuclear weapons.[10] The most important effect of this altered framing was that technology supplier regimes were established or strengthened on all forms of weapons and related technologies. Again, India was not invited into these groups, and the effect has been to deny India access to contemporary technologies.

This third period ended with two more serious slaps in India's face: the indefinite extension of the NPT in 1995 and the signing of a CTBT in 1996.[11] The decision in 1995 to extend the NPT made permanent a system from which India is excluded, and to which India has systematically objected since it was first signed. The damage India perceived to its self-perception and interests was made even worse by the signing in 1996 of a CTBT. India had pushed for a CTBT for more than forty years because it was an important step toward disarmament. Without

---

[10] For a more complete account of this change, see Mutimer, *The Weapon State: Proliferation and the Framing of Security* (Boulder: Lynne Rienner, 2000).

[11] For my account of the relationship between these two events and the Indian test of 1998, see Mutimer, "Testing Times: Of nuclear tests, test bans and the framing of proliferation," *Contemporary Security Policy* 23 (1) 2000, 1–23.

nuclear testing, the nuclear states would not be able to develop new weapons, and they would gradually lose confidence in the safety and reliability of the weapons they did have. These dual effects of the CTBT, therefore, should have created disarmament over a reasonable period. But by 1996, this logic no longer held, and the CTBT was seen as part of a non-proliferation regime, a regime India has so long opposed. What made this possible was the development of computer simulation technology, which allows the nuclear weapon states to check the reliability of their weapons by simulation—and may even let them develop new generations of warheads.[12]

The CTBT was the final taunt to India, and it responded by lashing out. This time India tested a series of nuclear explosives, and it announced that they were indeed nuclear weapon tests, not peaceful nuclear explosives. India has also been open in stating that it was trying to achieve respect. Consider the following statement from 1993, from a spokesman of the BJP: "Nuclear weapons will give us prestige, power, standing. An Indian will walk straight and talk straight when we have the bomb."

What has happened since the test supports the claim I tentatively advanced concerning the effect of standing up to bullies. The US, certainly, has shown considerably more respect for India. The deputy secretary of state at the time—Strobe Talbott—admitted that the US had not been giving India the respect it deserved. Talbott was the point man in the Clinton administration on India and the nuclear issue, as he led negotiations with India following the tests. India has also claimed to have received more high-level visits from the US—and, importantly, from others of the "West"—since the test than in the rest of its independent history.[13] Consider the following passage from a speech by the US undersecretary of state for political affairs, in December 1999: "Recognizing the potential for closer ties with India, and the increasing importance of India on the world stage in the next century, President Clinton has expressed a desire to travel there in 2000. That would be the first visit of a US president in over 20 years."

---

[12] Indeed the US has begun planning for the development of a new warhead, the first in nearly twenty years. At the beginning of March 2007, the Administration chose the design for the new warhead, awarding the project to the Livermore National Lab. The design will be based on a previously tested design, but then will be "tested" through simulations based on those earlier explosive tests. In other words, a new warhead will be possible without breaking the testing moratorium precisely because of the capacity to use simulation technologies.

[13] Reported to the author in a conversation with a senior Indian diplomat, Toronto, November 1999.

The treatment of India has continued under the present administration, reaching a high point in 2006 with the agreement on civil nuclear co-operation. Such co-operation should, of course, be impossible with a state in India's position, yet the agreement is making its way through the US process (and, of course, leading to this meeting). The agreement seems to indicate that the US has abandoned the goal of "rollback," and is accepting India as a *de facto* NWS—although this, of course, is not official policy. Such a claim, however, is supported by a central feature of the agreement, that certain of India's nuclear facilities are to be exempted from safeguarding; that is, precisely the relationship with the international monitors enjoyed by the NWS.

By Way of Conclusion

In the field of International Relations we commonly talk of states bullying one another, but generally that we mean merely that a powerful state is pushing around one less powerful and compelling to the latter to follow the former's interest. Bullying, therefore, has served merely as a label for the most clumsy and overt behaviour of states, but which is not qualitatively different from that which they pursue all the rest of the time. However, international relations has taken a reflexive turn in recent years, and the social rather than strategic character of state action has taken an increasingly important place in its arguments. What I have sought to do in this paper is explore the possibilities and limits of a social understanding of bullying as a metaphor for thinking about social relations among states. The story of US-Indian nuclear relations told through the lens provided by the bullying metaphor certainly seems plausible.[14] It is not a story that seems markedly at odds with the evidence, nor with the understandings we would expect of those relations from those familiar with them. Is the story useful, however, in a critical or analytic fashion, and does it suggest that a more sophisticated bullying metaphor, drawing on the theoretical underpinnings of social psychology, will be useful for international relations? I suggest, tentatively, that the answer to both questions is yes.

In the case of India and the US, the bullying metaphor draws particular attention to issues of respect and recognition in understanding the Indian decision to test nuclear weapons. The sophisticated bullying metaphor suggests that the tests are in part an attempt to alter the relations of *respect* among India, the US, and the broader international community. On this reading, the tests were produced in the ongoing relationship with the US,

---

[14] On the standards for judging interpretive storytelling in International Relations, see Mark Neufeld, *The Restructuring of International relations Theory* (Cambridge: CUP) and also Hidemi Suganami, "Agents, Structures, Narratives," *European Journal of International relations,* 5 (3) 1999, 365–86.

rather than in relation to Pakistan or China. Such ideas of respect and recognition are far from the understandings associated with the power-political conception of bullying, and of the conventional explanations of the Indian tests as a reaction to a dangerous strategic environment.

More broadly, the bullying metaphor draws attention to the multiple forms of power which circulate through world politics. Power is a notoriously ill-theorized concept in international relations, and the bullying metaphor provides a hook on which to hang a more complete understanding of social power. In this regard, in addition to the importance of status and recognition, bullying draws particular attention to the play of peers in power relations. A social conception of power, drawn from the bullying literature, would emphasize the place of peer involvement—through reinforcement, mimesis, and attitudes to the principals in social relations—in constituting the ongoing relations of power among subjects in global practices.

For Canada, this story of US-Indian relations as that of bully and victim locates us in a very specific way. Canada becomes part of this "peer group" supportive of the Americans' bullying behaviour. This is true generally given our place as one of the Western states that is broadly like-minded with the US, but rather more specifically as a member of the nuclear supplier groups that police access to advanced nuclear technology. It suggests that as we look to the future and our relationship with a nuclear-armed India, we need to keep the longer-term, world-order effects of our actions firmly in mind. In particular, Canada needs to work to create a context in which India is *included* in the broad regimes governing military technology, and included with a status commensurate to its place in the global military order. We must work in particular to avoid actions that tend to lead to further instances of *social exclusion* of India; that is, yet more moments of nuclear bullying.

Reconciling Indian Nuclear Co-operation and the International Non-proliferation Regime

Stephen I. Schwartz

What I will attempt to do in this essay is review some of the key findings or themes that emerge from the other conference presentations, and then offer observations that flow from these themes and my own research in this area.

But first, there is good news. While I will not go into tremendous detail here, suffice it to say that the non-proliferation regime, by and large, works. Nuclear proliferation is not inevitable. It is also important to point out that where proliferation is concerned, things could be much, much worse. It is easy to get caught up in the crisis *du jour* and forget that there were a number of times during the Cold War when tensions were higher, risks were greater, and the chances of a positive and peaceful outcome seemed quite remote.

So when it comes to the spread and potential use of nuclear weapons, is the world a more dangerous place than it was twenty years ago, shortly before the end of the Cold War? There is no simple answer to this question.

There are currently 27,000 nuclear weapons worldwide. As enormous as that figure is, it is 62 percent smaller than 1987, the year global nuclear stockpiles peaked at more than 70,000 weapons. Ninety-six percent of today's weapons are controlled by the US and Russia, the shrinking but still potent remnants of their Cold War-era arsenals. Based on this fact alone, one might conclude that the threat of nuclear war has diminished substantially too. It has, although the reduction in animosity did more to drive the reduction in weapons than vice-versa.

Nevertheless, 27,000 is still completely disproportionate to the threat faced by any country. If we could somehow divide just the firepower in the US nuclear arsenal into weapons equivalent in size to the one that destroyed Hiroshima on August 6, 1945—fifteen kilotonnes (equal to 15,000 tons of TNT), by today's standards a relatively small weapon—the US arsenal would consist of about 91,500 bombs. Detonated at the rate of one per second, it would take more than twenty-five hours to exhaust the entire stockpile. But as a bumper sticker from the 1980s put it, "It just takes one nuclear weapon to ruin your whole day."

Which brings us to the second criterion for measuring the level of danger—the number of nuclear-armed states. Twenty years ago there were seven—the US, the Soviet Union, the UK, France, China, Israel, and India. With the addition of Pakistan in 1998 and North Korea last year, the number is now nine, but it is important to note that Pakistan's nuclear program began more than thirty years ago and North Korea's nuclear ambitions stretch back to the 1950s.

Between 1987 and today, South Africa abandoned its covert nuclear program, dismantled the six weapons it had built, and signed the NPT. In addition, the Ukraine, Belarus, and Kazakhstan, which inherited significant parts of the former Soviet Union's nuclear arsenal upon the dissolution of that country, all agreed to return these weapons to Russia and become full members of the NPT. Nor should we forget that following the first Gulf War in 1991, the full extent of Iraq's nuclear program was uncovered by inspectors from the IAEA and was subsequently dismantled.

During a March 1963 press conference, President John F. Kennedy took a decidedly pessimistic line on the prospects for nuclear proliferation (Kennedy 1963):

> ...I am haunted by the feeling that by 1970, unless we are successful [in achieving a comprehensive nuclear test ban], there may be 10 nuclear powers instead of four, and by 1975, 15 or 20. With all of the history of war, and the human race's history unfortunately has been a good deal more war than peace, with nuclear weapons distributed all through the world, and available, and the strong reluctance of any people to accept defeat, I see the possibility in the 1970s of the President of the US having to face a world in which 15 or 20 or 25 nations may have these weapons.

Kennedy's fear was based on a secret study given to him the previous month by Secretary of Defense Robert S. McNamara, in which McNamara forecasted that by 1973 eight more states—China, Sweden, India, Australia, Japan, South Africa, Germany, and Israel—might obtain nuclear weapons and that soon thereafter many additional countries would do so as the costs to acquire a nuclear capability dropped dramatically.

That such dire predictions did not come to pass is remarkable considering that there have always been many more countries that could "go nuclear" than actually have. So what happened? Some states that fell under the US or Soviet nuclear umbrella chose not to develop programs of their own.

In others, leaders weighed the choice and decided that nuclear weapons were not in their national interest. Some conducted experiments but never made the leap to building weapons. And in at least two cases, Egypt and Iraq, sabotage undermined efforts to build the bomb.

But the most important development in constraining the spread of nuclear weapons was the enactment of the NPT in 1970. In return for a pledge not to acquire nuclear weapons, and a commitment by the five major nuclear powers to pursue negotiations to end the arms race "at an early date," and to nuclear disarmament, non-nuclear states gained access to nuclear technology for scientific research and energy production and, later, a certain measure of protection against a nuclear attack. Today, only four states—India, Israel, Pakistan, and North Korea—are not parties to the agreement, making it the most widely subscribed to international treaty in history (North Korea withdrew as a signatory in 2003, the first and only state to do so, but its status vis-à-vis the treaty has not been finalized).

Although the NPT and the subsequent agreements and organizations that have grown up around it are not perfect, they are preferable to the alternative—nuclear anarchy. Unfortunately, the international non-proliferation regime is under enormous strain, thanks to North Korea and Iran, and long-standing concerns of the non-nuclear parties to the NPT that the NWS are not adequately fulfilling their disarmament obligations. Several states are reconsidering their non-nuclear stance. Actions taken by the US—including refusing to ratify the CTBT, reneging on agreements reached in 2000 to strengthen the NPT, abandoning the 1972 Anti-Ballistic Missile Treaty in 2002, justifying the invasion of Iraq on the (erroneous) premise of needing to curtail advanced nuclear, chemical, and biological weapons programs, and approving an unprecedented nuclear co-operation agreement with India, granting it financial and technical rewards it could not otherwise achieve as an NPT outsider—have not helped.

If nuclear proliferation accelerates in the future, we may see some or all of the following occur:

(i)   Regional arms races, involving not just two adversaries (such as India and Pakistan) but their neighbours as well.

(ii)   Increasing potential for preventive or preemptive war as countries try to eliminate nuclear threats before they pose too great a danger.

(iii)   Rising risks of theft and/or accidental or deliberate use of nuclear weapons as more countries deploy nuclear weapons.

(iv)   The further weakening and possible collapse of the global non-proliferation regime.

We must do what we can to prevent any of these outcomes.

Of all the information provided in this conference's presentations, four things stood out for me. First was the number of missed opportunities over the years to establish closer nuclear ties with India while at the same time bolstering the non-proliferation regime. Second was the feeling that Canada was betrayed by India in the 1970s, something that we heard was more a perception among Canadian officials than a legal reality. Nevertheless, this has had important ramifications for relations between the two countries. Third, competition over the years between economic and security priorities tended to skew or undermine non-proliferation goals (something that has afflicted the US, particularly with regard to its relations with Pakistan). And finally, the steadfastness with which India has tried to secure the most advantageous position possible (this is to be expected, of course, but it is still worth bearing in mind when considering the present negotiations).

Based on these findings, I offer the following seven observations, with the caveat that I am not an expert in Canada-India relations, the civilian nuclear industry, or the US-India nuclear co-operation agreement:

(i)   There are clear advantages—to India and the world—in India investing more heavily in nuclear power. But there is no compelling reason to bypass the usual and well-established non-proliferation safeguards to make this a reality. Indeed, doing so would tend to undercut many of these benefits.

(ii)   Ironically, the measures being set aside by the pending US-India agreement were established in large measure as a response to India's 1974 nuclear test.

(iii)   Two wrongs don't make a right. The inequities of the NPT cannot and should not be resolved by granting India such extraordinary access. Perpetuating these inequities merely pushes down the road the issue of how to deal with states that seek nuclear weapons.

(iv)   At the same time, it is worthwhile to explore how to bring India more fully into the non-proliferation regime, along with the other outsiders. But we should build *on* the regime, not *around* it.

(v) The proliferation problems we face today are in large measure a consequence of the poorly-thought-out Atoms for Peace program of the 1950s. This is, of course, not a perfect analogy, but we need to be very careful not to repeat history.

(vi) For the US, using this agreement to make India a significant regional counterbalance to China is, in my opinion, a serious mistake. We made similar decisions and arrangements throughout the Cold War, and many proved shortsighted and harmful to US interests in the long term. We cannot and should not play favourites, because this will only codify existing disparities and create further resentment and weakening of the already weakened non-proliferation regime.

(vii) How will others (Iran, Israel, Pakistan, China, etc.) respond to the agreement should it be approved, and how do we avoid charges of hypocrisy or nuclear discrimination once again? The present proposed arrangement may only involve the US and India, but its repercussions extend worldwide.

In conclusion, I propose that rather than accepting this deal as a fait accompli, countries such as Canada should raise concerns now, before the US and India finalize their understanding of the agreement. Those concerns should be addressed and resolved by the NSG and the IAEA. Austria has recently questioned the wisdom of the agreement. Will Canada join her in working to set things right?

Fixing the problems with this agreement will not solve all the non-proliferation dilemmas that confront us. But a revised agreement that does not cast aside so much established precedent could prevent the development of many future problems and also make it possible to solve current and future ones more easily and in a more timely fashion.

India, the Global Nuclear Order and Canadian Policy Options

Karthika Sasikumar and Wade L. Huntley

The chapters in this volume have considered diverse aspects of new nuclear co-operation with India. In this conclusion, we attempt to draw out the major strands of the discussion, with particular attention to the implications for the policy choices of the Canadian government. We begin with a summary of developments in India's nuclear program. We then lay out the two positions—absolutist and revisionist—that have characterized the global response to the Indian program. This bipolar debate, we argue, is not only unproductive but has also obscured larger and more important questions. We then consider some of these questions, such as the centrality of the NPT in the non-proliferation order, the significance of "recognizing" India's nuclear weapons, and the relative weight of national interest and arms control for decision-makers in the United States. We end with a discussion of policy premises for Canada.

Current Status

India today is a nuclear weapons power. The country has been known, for several years now, to be capable of producing nuclear warheads and delivering them somewhat reliably. According to estimates recently published in the *Bulletin of the Atomic Scientists*, India currently has an arsenal of 50 to 60 nuclear warheads (Norris and Kristensen 2007). Moreover, the Indian government has formally adopted security policies explicitly relying upon nuclear deterrence, and claims to have incorporated nuclear weapons into operational military roles. India had a nuclear weapons capability well before the 1998 nuclear tests when it declared itself a Nuclear Weapon State.

The NPT, concluded in 1968, entailed a basic bargain: member states possessing nuclear weapons pledged to eliminate them, while member states without nuclear weapons pledged not to acquire them. The treaty stipulated that only the five countries that had conducted nuclear test explosions prior to 1967 could join as NWS. India was not one of those countries. Its 1974 "Peaceful Nuclear Explosion" (PNE) placed it in an awkward position with regards to the NPT which it denounced and rejected as discriminatory. However, since the Indian government did not overtly pursue weapons development, India's nuclear status was not prominent on the world's agenda.

Canadians felt especially aggrieved by India's PNE because the Indian nuclear program had been reaping the benefits from a Canadian nuclear aid agreement. In the ensuing storm the nuclear issue took on emotional hues. The frequent use of words like 'betrayal' in describing Indian actions testifies to the extent of this emotion.

Discussions of Indo-Canadian relations at the conference noted that in the years prior to 1974 Canadian diplomats appeared unwilling to ask hard questions about the eventual direction of the Indian nuclear program. There was a clear Canadian preference to take the Indian government's professions of "peaceful intent" at face value, and there was no full review of bilateral relations until 1973. The extensive but inconclusive post-1974 diplomatic exchanges between Indian and Canadian practitioners about the interpretation of the "peaceful uses" concept evince how far mutual understandings had diverged.

The reasons for this omission are of more than historical interest. As Canada attempts to formulate a new policy towards India today, similarities to the earlier period are striking. How much importance is given to India in the constellation of Canada's foreign relations, relative to other priorities? If policy-makers at the highest levels are not attentive to issues related to India, policy may drift. Did policy-makers turn a blind eye to warning signs in order to expediently sustain immediate collaboration, wishfully hoping darker consequences would not follow? Investing long-term thinking into short-term policy-making is always a challenge. In the 1950s, was it more convenient to stand by old decisions and commercial interests (most importantly, the fledgling AECL) than to re-consider the uses that India would make of nuclear aid? Today, AECL is once again in a precarious position, and requires foreign contracts for sustained viability, placing obvious pressure on policy-makers to allow, as Touhey put it, dollars to trump security concerns.

The decision by India to test a nuclear device in 1974 had a political fallout in Canada; the Canadian position on international nuclear safeguards was molded almost entirely by its sour experience with the Indians. As strategic or economic linkages faded, the nuclear issue came to dominate Canadian policy toward India. Consequently, after 1974 the irreconcilable differences on the nuclear issue undercut the larger bilateral relationship.

The feeling of betrayal still lingers among Canadian foreign policy elites. Those who were active in the non-proliferation area felt that their professional judgment had been called into question by the actions of the Indian government. Canada also felt that it was implicitly blamed by world opinion for supplying the reactor that was the origin of the fissile material in India's 1974 device. As Kapur points out, one tangible consequence was the transfer of questions of nuclear co-operation with India from regional experts to non-proliferation specialists. The altered internal balance of power within the Canadian foreign policy establishment was a lasting consequence of this episode of Canada's nuclear encounter with India.

Absolutist and Revisionist Positions

The nuclear test series at Pokhran in summer 1998, and the subsequent self-declaration of NWS status by the Indian Prime Minister, marked India's crossing of a key threshold: the aspiration that India might join the NPT as a NNWS was no longer a realistic policy objective. Since that point, the international community has faced the dilemma of how best to locate India within the global nuclear order.

In non-proliferation discussions even before 1998, the "absolutist" position on this question – holding out for Indian accession to the NPT as a NNWS and considering all Indian nuclear weapons activity illegitimate – has been increasingly countered by a "revisionist" position calling for prioritizing India's emerging global role over its NPT status.

The absolutist position is rooted in the premise that the NPT agreement represents, among its parties, a consensus that the objectives of non-proliferation, arms control and disarmament (NACD) supersede any shorter-term or tactical objectives that might be served by allowing nuclear capabilities to spread in a given context. In short, NACD objectives trump other priorities, including short-term national interest. The justifications of new nuclear co-operation with India by the current administration in the US, on the basis of promoting economic linkages or bolstering India's position vis-à-vis China, challenge this fundamental norm.

In the revisionist perspective (best represented by Ashok Kapur's contribution to this volume), discomfort with traditional NACD priorities derives in part from perceptions that existing NPT regime mechanisms are failing to cope with the panoply of issues today facing the non-proliferation regime generally, and specifically the new nuclear threats emerging in the post-Cold War nuclear era. The revisionist position notes India's "responsible" behavior on nuclear policy and nuclear proliferation matters, implicitly accepts the legitimacy of India as a NWS, and emphasizes the importance of engaging India across a range of international relations issues. In 1998 Canada's Lloyd Axworthy succinctly described the revisionist view as "new nuclear *realpolitik*" (Axworthy 1998). Revisionists advocate co-operation with India on the basis that this policy is in the national interest.

The contributions by Kapur and Touhey remind us that the 1950s and 1960s represented a time of great optimism about the transformative power of the atom. At this time, the modalities of international safeguards were still being worked out. Debates raged about the right to acquire fissile materials, to store or reprocess spent material, and to conduct tests for national security reasons. The issues resonate today, as the world is on the brink of a nuclear expansion once again. According to the World Nuclear Association 28 new reactors are under construction, 62 planned, and 160 proposed, and most are planned in Asia (Broad and Sanger 2006). Just as in the 1960s, questions about the efficacy and the fairness of the nuclear non-proliferation regime are being raised.

The prospect of an expanding global civil nuclear power sector, combined with the lessons of recent experiences with Iraq and Iran regarding the ease with which civil nuclear technologies have been diverted to military programs in the past, drives today's resurgent concern over safeguarding the nuclear fuel cycle. Even the IAEA has proposed that its safeguards system be replaced, or at least supplemented, with a global nuclear fuel bank. With respect to India, the chance to extend safeguards to at least some of India's nuclear power facilities is a non-proliferation plus – a principal reason the IAEA has supported the new nuclear co-operation initiative.

Skepticism about the NPT regime's ability to cope with the new challenges entailed by this nuclear boom – especially detection and punishment of regime outliers – drives the frustration of the Bush Administration with the regime generally. This reflects the administration's wider disillusionment with multilateral regimes, especially in the security realm. Instead, the Bush Administration has led development of multilateral voluntary arrangements like the Proliferation Security Initiative intended to circumvent what it sees as the paralysis of traditional non-proliferation structures in dealing with new challenges such as the spectre of nuclear terrorism.

At this conference, the roots of the absolutist view in the Canadian sense of betrayal and guilt were evident in the discussion of the history of India-Canada nuclear relations. Today, however, such perceptions are more than ever an impediment to practical policy-making toward India. In this sense, the Canadian position, for all its unique elements, brings home the global necessity of transcending the "absolutist" position that no longer offers a tenable strategy to define India's relationship to global non-proliferation.

The revisionist position has recognized this need. But the new posture it proposes, as displayed in the US-India nuclear co-operation agreement, goes beyond redefining India's role in the nuclear order – it seeks to reconstitute that order itself by disowning NACD objectives as a "trumping" global priority.

Beyond the Bipolar Debate

Larger questions are at issue than are reflected in this bipolar debate between absolutism and revisionism. What should be the world's objectives concerning nuclear weapons today? Is disarmament still relevant? Is the full range of NACD objectives evoked by the NPT regime still a "trumping priority" over near-term national interest-based policy?

These questions are separate from, and in a sense prior to, the question of whether the time has come to accept (*de facto* if not *de jure*) India's status as a nuclear weapons state. When framed this way, it is clear that the absolutist posture of simply ostracizing India over its nuclear weapons acquisition has been increasingly in tension with India's growing global status, the reality that it would not join the NPT as a NNWS, and the need for Indian collaboration with a range of global non-proliferation efforts, such as export controls. In world order terms, there is an imbalance between India's (unacknowledged) nuclear status and its (rising) power status; the non-proliferation regime (like any international regime) has to adapt to changing political realities if it is going to remain relevant and useful.

Both the absolutist and revisionist positions implicitly share the premise that nuclear engagement of India necessarily undermines the NPT regime as now constituted. The absolutist position, sensing that such engagement is inevitable, seeks to "minimize the damage" to the regime, while the revisionist position appreciates the pressure that the India deal puts on the regime to move beyond antiquated disarmament objectives. This premise that nuclear engagement of India necessarily undermines global NACD objectives may be challenged on two fronts.

First, the disarmament objectives enshrined in the NPT are far from antiquated, as the revisionist position holds. The virtual elimination of the threat of large-scale nuclear war between heavily armed superpowers has reduced the overall level of the perceived dangers of nuclear weapons in and of themselves (which many now localize onto particularly dangerous states and non-state actors). Ironically, this reduced perception of nuclear risk drains the urgency from the objective of ultimate nuclear disarmament. But that objective remains as relevant today as it has ever been – as evoked in the recent call by four prominent US leaders to undertake practical measures toward realizing "the vision of a world free of nuclear weapons" (Shultz, Perry, and Nunn 2007).

Secondly, the premise that the goals of global nuclear disarmament and nuclear engagement of India are antithetical is specious also in bypassing the potential for India to be a positive participant in the global nuclear order rather than an outsider. Revisionists are right to emphasize that circumstances have changed considerably since the Cold War. India is today a regional power, and despite decades of political turmoil and poverty it remains a vibrant secular democracy. India now aims to fully express its independence in foreign policy and has aspirations to become a global power. Increasingly, India is, as Keeley evoked, the "big empty spot" in the global nuclear order.

Meanwhile, the NPT regime itself has also changed over the years. The regime today encompasses norms and practices extending well beyond the treaty itself. The role of the IAEA—which preceded the NPT in existence and which includes India as a core active member—is more central to the regime than ever. Thus, the opportunities to strengthen that regime by bringing India more fulsomely into it have never been greater.

Yet absolutists correctly point out that if India is allowed unconditionally to join the five NWS recognized by the regime, countries that are close to the nuclear "tipping point" will be convinced that it pays to go nuclear and present the world with a *fait accompli*. In this view, India must make fundamental concessions that will not only guarantee that its own program will be rolled back, but also signal to other nuclear hopefuls that defiance of non-proliferation norms carries ultimate costs.

If the right deal with India can promote non-proliferation goals, there need not be a contradiction with either position. At the start of the conference, Michael Blackmore posed the question: "Will India re-align its foreign policy with broad Western interests if accorded civil nuclear co-operation?" It appears that India's foreign policy priorities are more or less compatible with Western interests at the moment. India has sharp disagreements with G-8 countries on trade issues, and it is keeping its options open by forging issue-based alliances with Russia and China in a putative "strategic triangle". Yet, Indian policy-makers are fully aware of the importance of being seen as a responsible rising power in the global system and are unlikely to challenge the system's basic norms. Moreover, for the next decade or so, India seems to have decided to focus on economic growth and consolidation. India's posture toward Iran has certainly come closer to US desires since the advent of the nuclear deal; that trend would probably reverse if the nuclear deal were now to fall through.

Thus, elements of both the absolutist and revisionist outlooks have merits; yet the positions speak past each other, overlooking opportunities for synthetic solutions to current challenges. Debate limited to only the bipolar absolutist and revisionist positions truncates the real range of choices relative to defining India's future global role in the nuclear order and in world politics generally. Transcending this opposition, the appropriate question with respect to India is not *whether* it should be engaged on nuclear matters, but *how*.

And if, as critics claim, new nuclear co-operation with India as currently envisioned undermines broader NACD objectives, the appropriate question becomes: how can we fashion an engaged role for India that *promotes* those objectives? How can the world do better than absolutist adherence to abstinence from any nuclear engagement with India? How can a global consensus on the political as well as technical terms for such engagement be established?

Bringing India into the Club

In the conference's discussions, a general consensus emerged around the desirability of fashioning a new relationship between India and the non-proliferation regime that would serve both sides better than the *status quo*. But conference participants disagreed on a number of specific issues concerning the necessary details of a "win-win" arrangement and whether such an outcome remains politically feasible.

One strand in our discussion naturally revolved around the centrality of the NPT. Some suggested that if the NPT was only a means to the end of NACD, it may be time for the international community to look for other measures that did not involve multilateral institutions. One participant challenged the idea that the NPT has been instrumental in preventing proliferation, asserting that its putative success may be an instance of correlation without causation. Others countered that the NPT was a symbol of serious normative commitments made by both NWS and NNWS, and a collectively-stated objective. Therefore, tampering with it would send out the signal that such commitments no longer had value. They maintained that the US, foremost among the NWS, wants to detach the NPT from the non-proliferation norm because that would relieve it of its own Article VI obligations.

A second strand addressed the question of terminology. Discussions of James Keeley's and Ernie Regehr's proposals to create a new "third" status for India (and the other two non-NPT nuclear-armed states— Pakistan and Israel) wrestled directly with the problem of fashioning a positively contributory role for India. In particular, Regehr's assessment of India's current performance relative to a set of criteria parallel to those of the NWS, and his suggestion that India's search for legitimation could be harnessed to oblige it to accept such parallel responsibilities, generated discussion not only on criteria definitions but also on the desirability of developing such generalizable standards for a "third" status category at all. Would such "benchmarks" encourage Pakistan and Israel to follow India's lead in better embracing non-proliferation norms? Or would such criteria legitimate exceptionalism *per se*, beyond the India-specific case, unnecessarily undercutting disarmament objectives? The ensuing discussion highlighted the core issue of the *terms* by which India would be allowed entry into the global nuclear order as a possessor of nuclear weapons.

A third strand in the discussion raised suggestions for improvements in current non-proliferation arrangements. For example, Keeley noted that the IAEA, which would be responsible under the India-US agreement for inspections of Indian nuclear facilities, is unable at present to safeguard each reactor that is put under its authority. One measure that would help constrain India's capability would be increased funding to the IAEA, enabling it to inspect all the safeguarded reactors.

From this perspective, the problem with the current deal is not that it breaches the absolutist rejection of any nuclear dealings with India. The problem is that the deal creates a *less* responsible role for India, rather than a more responsible role. Nuclear co-operation with India can and should be developed in consonance with the goal of sustaining the NACD "trumping priority" implicit in NPT regime's foundational precepts.

Such a role was envisioned in the proposals, noted above, to create a "third category" status designation for non-NPT nuclear-armed states. Terms of that status would provide the opportunity and criteria for these states to make arms control and disarmament commitments equivalent to those of the NPT's five acknowledged nuclear-armed states (such as permanently ceasing nuclear testing and fissile material production). Such a role would acknowledge the transitions of norms and power relationships defining the post-Cold War world, but retain the objective of sustaining global consensus on the goal of nuclear disarmament.

That the current deal does not create such a role flows directly from the revisionist motivations that the Bush Administration brought to its forging. The administration has rejected an overarching disarmament vision in favour of embracing indefinite nuclear weapons possession by the United States and other "responsible" states combined with non-proliferation and counterproliferation against "rogue" states like North Korea and Iran. The administration's policy postures have openly questioned the effectiveness of multilateral arms control processes generally, and have specifically dismissed the relevance of American nuclear weapons practices to its non-proliferation objectives – effectively disowning the linkage between arms control and non-proliferation that defines the NPT in the eyes of most of its state parties (Huntley 2006).

With this orientation, the Bush Administration's approach to negotiating new nuclear co-operation with India simply did not take bolstering the non-proliferation regime as a core motivation. There is ample evidence that the negotiators on the US side were handicapped by the pressure to produce an agreement with the Indians. Indeed, many advocates of the deal in the US consider it a means to usefully circumscribe the role of the non-proliferation regime in defining the global nuclear weapons order.

Indian diplomats were quick to leap through this window of opportunity. After 1998, the Indian government has taken pains to highlight its restraint in transferring nuclear technology to other would-be nuclear states. As the large Indian market opened up, and Indian companies began participating in global supply chains, India acquired new friends among commercial interests in the US. Concerns about terrorism are another basis on which India has successfully sought rapprochement with the US. The idea that India could serve as a counterweight in Asia to an increasingly powerful China has been particularly convincing to those American elites inclined to follow *realpolitik*. As Rajaraman's contribution notes, the end result was a very good deal from India's point of view.

Unfortunately, absolutist opposition to the deal, depicting any nuclear dealing with India as compromising global disarmament objectives, forsook the opportunity to direct that engagement toward reinforcing global disarmament objectives instead. A better deal may have been possible if opposition to the initial US-India announcement of July 2005 had focused on fine-tuning the deal rather than resisting it outright. Indeed, long before the Bush Administration's initiative, NPT defenders and disarmament advocates could have been more proactive in recognizing the eventual need to incorporate India into the global nuclear order in some fashion.[1] But this is history. To address the policy-making challenges Canada and other countries face today, the relevant question is whether a better (i.e. disarmament-promoting) deal *remains possible now.*

Endgame on the Nuclear Deal

Under what circumstances could a deal that bridges the absolutist and revisionist positions still be achieved? Several factors bear on answering this question.

Most central is Blackmore's question concerning what further commitments can realistically be sought from India at this stage to move it closer to the international nuclear mainstream. In the conference discussions, the rationale behind India's insistence on exempting the fast breeder reactor program from safeguards received specific attention. Participants with experience in this field claimed that Indian nuclear scientists are wary of the red tape that would come with international safeguards on a fledgling program, suggesting that keeping the breeder program out of the purview of the IAEA would be a priority for the Indians. Another issue related to India's desire to reserve the right to "corrective measures" in the event of an interruption in fuel supply to safeguarded reactors, and whether this could be reconciled with the requirement for India to place facilities and materials under safeguards in perpetuity.

Participants also discussed how public debate in India has revealed considerable opposition to the US-India initiative from the nuclear scientific establishment and from across the political spectrum. Opposition parties on both the Right (the nationalist Bharatiya Janata Party) and the Left (the Communist parties, who are at present members of the ruling coalition) are keeping the government under scrutiny. Several participants cautioned that seeking to add more conditions to the deal now would turn opinion in India against accepting any sort of international safeguards. Although assertiveness on the nuclear issue has not been an election-winning issue in the past, perceived "backsliding" on the accomplishments of Indian scientists and the carefully protected nuclear deterrent capability now will likely be punished at the ballot. Since the original India-US deal was worded rather loosely, many Indian commentators view the current negotiations with the US and the enabling legislation passed by the Congress as attempts to slide back the gains of 2005. If the original deal had had more stringent provisions, the task of

---

[1] As Keeley's contribution notes, a study prepared by the Canadian Department of Foreign Affairs in November 2004 anticipated the utility of such efforts.

the American negotiators would be easier. The reflexive anti-Americanism of the past, coupled with the self-assurance of a growing economy and a vibrant polity, make India a tough negotiator.

In the US, opposition by long-standing Congressional arms control advocates to the initial July 2005 agreement eroded as lobbying by India-related interests complemented the Bush Administration's own efforts to win support for necessary legislation to ratify the deal. By the time key legislation faced votes in the fall of 2006, widespread support was assured and what division remained on the issue transected the Republican-Democratic party divide. Yet, the legislation authorizing President Bush to conclude a final agreement (the Hyde Act) included several provisions, such as linking nuclear fuel provision to continued cessation of Indian nuclear testing, to which India has since objected. On the one hand, the ascension of Democratic majorities in both houses of Congress, combined with the President's own plummeting stature, will severely limit the administration's capacity to extract any further Congressional concessions toward its position on the India nuclear deal for the rest of its term. On the other hand, the Indian nuclear deal is unlikely to be the issue on which the Democrats directly challenge the executive.

Consequently, the remaining locus at which efforts to recast nuclear cooperation with India to promote rather than retard global NACD objectives might be undertaken is the NSG. The Hyde Act requires that the NSG consent to an agreement with India, requiring concurrence of each of its forty-five members. Many of these countries are not crucially concerned about India, and their decisions will be greatly influenced by the policies adopted by the NWS, and other influential states like Canada and Germany. As for the NWS, Russia and France have already expressed great interest in working with India on civil nuclear power projects. In fact, these two countries have already run into criticism for their alleged violations of NSG rules in dealing with India.

China, while obviously unsympathetic to India's nuclear ambitions, will also be influenced by the larger bilateral relationship with India. That relationship has been steadily improving for the last seven years or so, marked last year by a historic Memorandum of Understanding on defence issues. While Chinese publications have expressed disapproval of US attempts to bolster India and encircle China, the disapproval has been muted enough to convince Indian policy-makers that the key to securing Chinese acquiescence is to push forward co-operation on other issues, especially the burgeoning trade relationship.[2] China may also restrain its objections at the NSG for larger geopolitical reasons, such as avoiding a direct confrontation with the US and its allies at this time and on this issue, which would draw renewed attention to its own nuclear dealings with Pakistan. The most likely scenario is that China will press for a criteria-based approach—in order to open the door to an agreement with Pakistan—rather than a one-time exception solely for India (Bagchi 2006). Australia and Germany have already expressed interest in nuclear commerce with India, with the latter actively discussing uranium sales in New Delhi (Anon 2006a). South Africa, a leader of disarmament-minded states and the developing countries, has agreed to help India in the NSG (Khare 2006a).

Canadian Policy Options

What does all this mean for Canadian policy on nuclear co-operation with India? A first premise is the inconvenient fact that Canada matters far less in India's eyes than it did in 1974. With the advent of the nuclear deal, the focus in the Indian foreign policy establishment has shifted to recalibrating the relationship with the US. Relations between the US and India were for many years poisoned by the nuclear issue, and now that it has been brought into the open, dialogue has become constructive. Today India is eager to participate in a new US-led nuclear order as a responsible and legitimate possessor of nuclear weapons. Canada is not a major priority, and India is less tolerant than ever of Canadian lectures on non-proliferation.[3]

Just as the India-US nuclear deal of 2005 was the culmination of years of preceding relationship-building, any progress in India-Canada nuclear relations will have to be built on a solid foundation of bilateral ties in other areas. Blackmore posed the question: What implications might Canada's decision on the nuclear co-operation agreement have for its broader relationship with India? This begs a more fundamental question:

---

[2] According to the Economist Intelligence Unit, in 2005 China became the second most important export market for Indian goods, and surpassed the US as a source of Indian imports. In 2005, India-China trade increased by 37% over the previous year to touch $18.7 billion. Just three years earlier in 2002 the total volume of bilateral trade was a paltry $5 billion Aiyar, Pallavi. 2006. India-China trade: a long road ahead. *Hindu*, 7 September.

[3] Canada does not have much economic leverage with India. Canada currently accounts for only 0.6% of India's imports. Although Canadian exports to India rose by 20% in 2006 over the previous year, they still lag behind total growth in Indian imports (27%). Canadian investment in India is only $250 million USD out of a total Foreign Direct Investment of $6.7 billion Poloz, Stephen S. 2007. *Will Canada-India trade blossom?* Export Development Canada, 29 March 2006 [cited 20 August 2007]. Available from http://www.edc.ca/english/docs/ereports/commentary/publications_9754.htm.

will either country hold the improvement of relations hostage to concessions on the nuclear issue? Or might it be wiser for Canadian policy-makers to work on the broader relationship first? India has adopted a highly pragmatic and segmented approach to China, a country with which it has had many inflammatory quarrels, and engaged in combat in 1962. It is hard to believe that India would sacrifice the opportunity to improve relations with Canada for purely ideological reasons. Can Canada do the same?

A principal difficulty is that Canada following such a course would appear to impinge, in its own eyes and in the eyes of the world, on Canada's commitment to its longstanding NACD goals. It is hard for many to believe, as was evidenced in the discussion, that Canada could turn its back on its support for multilateral arms control measures by endorsing a bilateral agreement that could conceivably lead to a larger stockpile of nuclear warheads in India. Sustaining an avid prioritization of NACD objectives globally while minimizing the import of these objectives in the bilateral relationship with India would be a delicate balancing act that would require an active accommodation by India to succeed.

This dilemma comes to a head in considering how Canada might approach its role in the forthcoming debate over nuclear co-operation with India at the NSG. Ideally, Canada could use its position at the NSG to insist upon a better nuclear arrangement with India that would retain and feature the global normative consensus on the priority of NACD objectives over specific national interests. Canada would proactively lead a coalition of like-minded NSG states behind this initiative.

But this ideal may not be practical. Prominent Canadian obstructionism could undercut efforts to slowly regenerate broader bilateral relations with India. Canada might also find itself hard-pressed to find NSG partners willing to be equally prominent on the issue. Not least of all, the political cost to the US-Canada bilateral relationship would certainly be tremendous. Finally, a Canadian government undertaking such a policy could not expect to benefit from an upsurge in domestic support, as most Canadians are not moved by the issue. In fact, an NSG opposition might paint Canada as being inflexible and impractical on non-proliferation issues; or, worse, it could risk undercutting the effectiveness of the NSG itself, a consent-based process short of a treaty regime that depends on the continued concord of its members.

In short, in seeking to find ways to pursue a new engagement of India that also promotes global NACD goals, Canada needs to carefully seek to avoid policy directions that would achieve neither of these ends – the "lose-lose" flip side of the "win-win" opportunity outlined above. This will require establishing a clear longer-term vision but applying it flexibly and responsively rather than dogmatically and insularly.

Canada can and should press for an improved deal among NSG member states, but in a measured manner, continually cognizant of the boundaries of the politically possible and focused on the deeper goal of re-engaging *all* the nuclear-armed states with the aspiration of global nuclear disarmament. On the question of nuclear dealings with non-NPT members, Canada can stress the importance of generalized criteria with international backing that ensure a positive contribution to longstanding NACD goals (versus simply extending to Pakistan what has already been granted India). In the NSG and beyond, Canada can undertake active and sustained "backdoor diplomacy" aimed at strengthening multilateral NACD mechanisms, including the NPT regime. Where possible, Canada can utilize its unique relationship with the US to urge policy-makers in both US parties to retain global NACD goals as a "trumping priority" in US security policy.

What about India? Can Canada rebuild a broader relationship with India, and even co-operate on nuclear issues, without impinging on Canadian NACD priorities? The answer is yes, but much will depend on India's willingness to establish terms with Canada that may differ from those it is building with the US, which in turn depends on what unique benefits Canada can bring to the relationship.

For example, Seethapathy's contribution suggests that a technical and commercial partnership on CANDU technology could be one possible foundation on which to situate future India-Canada nuclear co-operation. Indian technocrats and scientists have become expert in handling the CANDU design, and they could collaborate with Canada in installing or maintaining this type of reactor in other countries. Indian scientists and engineers, long obliged by global sanctions to concentrate on fixing problems common to the CANDU reactor model, can now provide commercially significant services for these reactors. Canada's AECL has recently produced a new design, the Advanced CANDU, that is the basis of a concerted sales effort, with India being one potential customer (Webster 2006). But a broader partnership with India could also contribute to the wider attractiveness of the CANDU if Indian scientists can come up with a cheaper service plan than the current, prohibitively expensive maintenance schedule for the reactor.

Canada can pursue such opportunities, but should do so in a manner that ensures that its own nuclear dealings with India promote global disarmament goals in all the ways that the current US-India deal does not.

In other words, if it cannot improve the terms of that deal sufficiently, Canada ought nevertheless to hold itself to a higher standard.

Retaining that higher standard may mean Canada seeks terms for its own dealings that India could prove unwilling to abide by, resulting in Canada having no nuclear co-operation with India at all. But a nuclear dead-end need not impinge on rebuilding India-Canada relations more widely. As noted earlier, India has shown in its relations with China a capacity for pragmatism and constructiveness quarantining divisive issues to allow the broader relationship to move forward. India's stakes with Canada are lower; but with agile diplomacy offering due respect for India's global position, Canada could establish similar atmospherics. In short, Canada need not shed its commitment to global disarmament in order to put its relationship with India on a new footing. Canada need only clear away the sense of betrayal that lingers in policy dispositions. Bureaucratically, this goal would be advanced by returning South Asia specialists to the forefront of policy-making, while still incorporating the input of non-proliferation experts (and so helping overcome the culture of compartmentalization within government departments that several conference participants noted).

For Canada, like the other members of the NSG, many policy decisions await the details of the India-US deal to be finalized. There remain several stages that the deal still has to pass through before it can become a reality—India has to sign a safeguards agreement with the IAEA, the NSG has to approve the one-time exemption for India, and then the US Congress has to approve the start of civil nuclear commerce with India. Although the endgame of the process is at hand, uncertainties remain as to the final disposition of the deal, and a small possibility persists that the deal could collapse entirely. Even greater uncertainties loom concerning the implications and consequences of new nuclear co-operation with India once it culminates. Hence, above all Canadian policy should remain nimble and prepared for divergent courses of events. A renewed commitment to Canada's longstanding reputation for advancing the vision of a world free of the dangers of nuclear weapons would provide the orienting roadmap that enables such flexibility to be proactive and opportunistic rather than reactive and self-defeating.

Contributors

Michael Blackmore is currently a Senior Policy Officer in the Nuclear Non-Proliferation and Disarmament Division of the Department of Foreign Affairs and International Trade Canada (DFAIT). He has previously served at the Canadian High Commission in Kuala Lumpur, Malaysia (2001-2004) and Seoul, Republic of Korea (2004-2006), where he was concurrently accredited to the Democratic People's Republic of Korea (DPRK). Previous headquarters assignments include the Japan Division, the International Summits Division (APEC), the Regional Security and Peacekeeping Division, as well as a one-year assignment as the Executive Assistant to the Assistant Deputy Minister (and G8 Political Director), International Security Branch. Mr. Blackmore holds a BA (honours) from the University of Victoria and an MA from the Norman Paterson School of International Affairs at Carleton University.

Wade Huntley is Director of the Simons Centre for Disarmament and Non-Proliferation Research at the Liu Institute for Global Issues, UBC. Dr. Huntley was previously an Associate Professor at the Hiroshima Peace Institute in Hiroshima, Japan, and has served as Director of the Global Peace and Security Program at the Nautilus Institute for Security and Sustainable Development. Huntley's areas of expertise include international security, nuclear non-proliferation and arms control, political relations in the Asia-Pacific region, and political theory. He has published work addressing issues including nuclear developments in East and South Asia, US missile defense ambitions and deterrence policies, the relationship of democracy and peace, and philosophies of science. He received his Ph.D. in political science from the University of California at Berkeley in 1993.

Ashok Kapur is Emeritus Professor at the Department of Political Science at the University of Waterloo, and was most recently Chair of the Department. Author of over thirty refereed articles and eight books, his most recent work is *Pokhran and After: India's Nuclear Weapons Capability*, and *Regional Security Structures in Asia* (2003) among other works on the subcontinent. He received his PhD from Carleton University.

James F. Keeley is Professor in the Political Science Department at the University of Calgary. His research interests are in the theory of international regimes and nuclear non-proliferation. His recent work in these areas has concentrated on developments in International Atomic Energy Agency safeguards, including the possible use of satellite imagery. He has also developed a list of over 1450 (as of 1998) bilateral civilian nuclear co-operation agreements. His safeguards research and publications have been conducted in the context of research contracts with the Department of Foreign Affairs and International Trade.

David Mutimer is the Deputy Director of the York Centre for International and Security Studies and Associate Professor of Political Science at York University. His research considers issues of contemporary international security through lenses provided by critical social theory, as well as inquiring into the reproduction of security in and through popular culture. Much of that work has focused on weapons proliferation as a reconfigured security concern in the post-cold war era, and his book on the subject, *The Weapon State: Proliferation and the Framing of Security* was published in 2000. More recently he has turned his attention to the politics of the global war on terror, and of the regional wars around the world presently being fought by Canada and its allies.

R. Rajaraman is a theoretical physicist at Jawaharlal Nehru University, New Delhi. He obtained his PhD from Cornell University 1963. Over four decades, he has taught and /or done research at, among other places, Cornell University, the Institute for Advanced Study at Princeton, Harvard University, M.I.T, Stanford University, and the Indian Institute for Science at Bangalore. In addition he has also been writing and giving talks about the dangers of nuclear weapons. Often in collaboration with the arms control group at Princeton University, he has worked on a variety of problems including the need for a declared De-Alert status, the wisdom of acquiring Early Warning and missile defense systems, the dangers of nuclear weapon accidents, theft and unauthorized launches, and the possibilities for nuclear civil defense in South Asia.

Ernie Regehr, O.C., LL.D., is Co-Founder and now Senior Policy Advisor of Project Ploughshares, and Adjunct Associate Professor in Peace and Conflict Studies at Conrad Grebel University College, University of Waterloo. His publications on peace and security issues include books, monographs, journal articles, newspaper and magazine articles, conference papers, working papers, and Parliamentary briefs. He has served as an NGO representative and expert advisor on a number of Government of Canada delegations to multilateral disarmament forums, including Review Conferences of the Nuclear Non-Proliferation Treaty.

Among current appointments, he is a Commissioner on the World Council of Churches Commission on International Affairs and on the Board of Directors of the Africa Peace Forum based in Nairobi. In 2003 Regehr was appointed an Officer of the Order of Canada.

Karthika Sasikumar is a Postdoctoral Fellow at the Simons Centre for Disarmament and Non-Proliferation at the University of British Columbia. She completed her M.Phil. at Jawaharlal Nehru University, New Delhi (1999) and a Ph.D. in International Relations at Cornell University (2006). Her dissertation explores the interaction between India and the international nuclear non-proliferation order, and its implications for the emerging global counter-terrorism regime. Her major field is International Relations and her research interests are in International Relations theory, international security regimes in nuclear weapons, space, and South Asia.

Stephen I. Schwartz is Editor of the *Nonproliferation Review* published by the Center for Nonproliferation Studies at the Monterey Institute of International Studies. Before becoming Editor, he served as the Publisher and Executive Director of the *Bulletin of the Atomic Scientists*, and as a Guest Scholar with the Foreign Policy Studies Program at the Brookings Institution where he directed the U.S. Nuclear Weapons Cost Study Project. He writes and speaks regularly on nuclear policy matters and is an expert on many aspects of nuclear weapons, including the history and costs of the U.S. nuclear weapons program; weapons research, development, testing, production, and deployment; nuclear doctrine and strategy; command and control; missile defenses; and nuclear proliferation and disarmament. He is the author of numerous articles and the editor and co-author of *Atomic Audit: The Costs and Consequences of U.S. Nuclear Weapons Since 1940.*

Ravi Seethapathy is the Chair of the Canadian Advisory Council of the Shastri Indo-Canadian Institute (a binational institute of 58 Canadian/Indian universities funded by the governments of Canada and India). He is also a member of the Public Policy Advisory Board of the Pearson Shoyama Institute, a think-tank devoted to facilitating the involvement of a wide cross-section of Canadians in policy development, and a past President of the Indo-Canada Chamber of Commerce. He co-authored the Canada-India Science & Technology Mapping study for the federal government. He holds an MBA from York University, an M.Eng in Electrical Engineering from the University of Toronto and a B.Tech (Hons) from the Indian Institute of Technology.

Ryan Touhey has recently completed his doctorate at the University of Waterloo and is a reseacher for the Department of Foreign Affairs

Historical Section and a part-time lecturer at the University of Ottawa, Department of History. His research examines Canada's foreign relations with India beginning with Canada's attitudes towards post-1947 decolonization and the founding of the new Commonwealth to the collapse of bilateral relations in 1976 due to diverging attitudes on nuclear proliferation. He was a Shastri Institute Doctoral Fellow at the school of Canadian Studies at Jawaharlal Nehru University in 2003-2004. He is the author of 'Canadian and Indian Relations: A Historical Appreciation' in 'Canada's Global Engagement and Relations with India' edited by Christopher Raj.

References

Aiyar, Pallavi. 2006. India-China trade: a long road ahead. *Hindu*, 7 September.

Anon. 1998a. Investors see vast opportunities in India. *Hindu*, 6 June.

Anon. 1998b. Vajpayee finds US action discriminatory. *Hindu*, 9 November.

Anon. 2006. *Australia Considers Nuclear Exports to India* Nuclear Threat Initiative, 25 September 2006a [cited 25 September 2006].

Anon. 2007. *Signing test ban treaty may get NSG nod for N-deal* Rediff.com, 15 December 2006b [cited 2 August 2007]. Available from http://www.rediff.com/cms/print.jsp?docpath=//news/2006/dec/15ndeal.htm.

Anon. 2007. India bans nuclear exports to Iran. *BusinessWeek*, 21 February.

Arms Control Association. 2006. An Open Letter to Mohamed El Baredei, Director-General of the International Atomic Energy Agency.

Axworthy, Lloyd. 1998. India's Nuclear Testing: Implications for Nuclear Disarmament and the Nuclear Non-proliferation Regime, edited by D. o. F. A. a. I. Trade: Department of Foreign Affairs and International Trade, Government of Canada.

Bagchi, Indrani. 2006. N-deal may run into Chinese wall at NSG. *Times of India*, 6 June.

Bagla, Pallava. 2006. The Fast Breeder Programme just cannot be put on the civilian list. *Indian Express*, February 8.

Boese, Wade. 2006. Nuclear Suppliers Updated on US-Indian Deal. *Arms Control Today* 36 (9).

Boese, Wade. 2007. Slow Start in 2007 for U.S. Indian Nuclear Deal. *Arms Control Today*.

Bothwell, Robert. 1988. *Nucleus: The History of Atomic Energy of Canada Limited*. Toronto: University of Toronto Press.

Broad, William J., and David E. Sanger. 2006. Restraints Fray and Risks Grow as Nuclear Club Gains Members. *New York Times*, 15 October.

Bunn, Matthew, and Anthony Wier. 2006. Securing the Bomb 2006. In *Project on Managing the Atom. Commissioned by the Nuclear Threat Initiative.* Cambridge, MA: John F. Kennedy School of Government, Harvard University.

Chaffee, Devon, and Jim Wurst. 2002. Strengthening existing nuclear weapon-free zones.

Cohen, Avner , and Thomas Graham Jr. 2004. An NPT for non-members. *Bulletin of the Atomic Scientists* 40-44.

Donaghy, Greg. 2007. Nehru's Reactor: The Origins of Indo-Canadian Nuclear Cooperation, 1955-59. In *Canada's Global Engagements and Relations with India,* edited by C. Raj and A. Nafey. New Delhi: Manak Publications.

du Preez, Jean, and Sergio Duarte. 2006. Keeping the NPT Together: A Thankless Job in a Climate of Mistrust. *Nonproliferation Review* 13 (1):11-12.

Federation of American Scientists. 2002. Nuclear weapons -- India.

Foreign Affairs Canada. 2004. Weapons of Mass Destruction Verification and Compliance: Challenges and Responses The Weapons of Mass Destruction Commission.

Huntley, Wade L. 2006. Threats all the way down: US Strategic Initiatives in a Unipolar World. *Review of International Studies.*

Huntley, Wade L., and Karthika Sasikumar, eds. 2006. *Nuclear Cooperation with India: New Challenges, New Opportunities.* Vancouver, BC: Simons Centre for Disarmament and Non-Proliferation Research.

India Cabinet Committee on Security. 2003. The Cabinet Committee on Security reviews operationalization of India's nuclear doctrine, edited by C. C. o. Security.

India Department of Atomic Energy. 2005. Implementation of the India-United States Joint Statement of July 18, 2005: India's Separation Plan.

India Prime Minister's Office. 2007. *PM's Statement on US visit in Parliament, July 29* Prime Minister's Office, Government of India, 29 July 2005 [cited 1 July 2007]. Available from http://pmindia.nic.in/speech/content4print.asp?id=155.

India Prime Minister's Office. *Statement of PM in Rajya Sabha on the India-US Nuclear Agreement, August 17* Prime Minister's Office, Government of India, 17 August 2006a [cited. Available from http://pmindia.nic.in/parl/pcontent.asp?id=30.

India Prime Minister's Office. 2007. *Suo-motu Statement by the PM on Civil Nuclear Energy Cooperation with the United States, February 27* Prime Minister's Office, Government of India, 27 February 2006b [cited 22 July 2007]. Available from http://pmindia.nic.in/speech/content.asp?id=284.

Kennedy, John F. 1963. News Conference 52, 21 March 1963: John F. Kennedy Museum and Library.

Khare, Harish. 2006a. South Africa backs nuclear deal. *Hindu*, 3 October.

Khare, Harish. 2006b. South Africa backs nuclear deal. *The Hindu*, 3 October.

Kimball, Daryl G. 2007. *US Proposal for Changes to Nuclear Suppliers Group (NSG) Guidelines Circulated March 2006* Arms Control Association, 27 March 2006 [cited 22 June 2007]. Available from http://www.armscontrol.org/projects/india/20060327_DraftNS GProposal.asp.

Klug, Foster. 2006. Senate endorses US-India nuclear deal. *Washington Post, Associated Press*, 16 November.

Malanczuk, Peter. 1997. *Akehurst's Modern Introduction to International Law*. London: Routledge.

Martin, Paul. 1985. *A Very Public Life: So Many Worlds, Volume II*. Toronto: Deneau Publishers.

Mian, Zia, A.H. Nayyar, R. Rajaraman, and M.V. Ramana. 2006. Fissile Materials in South Asia: The Implications of the US-India Nuclear Deal: International Panel on Fissile Materials.

Mishra, Archana. 2007. *India test-fires nuclear-capable missile* ABC News, 19 November 2006 [cited 2 August 2007]. Available from http://abcnews.go.com/International/wireStory?id=2665247&C MP=OTC-RSSFeeds0312.

Natural Resources Defense Council. 2007. *Table of Indian Nuclear Forces, 2002* Natural Resources Defense Council, 25 November 2002 [cited 29 July 2007]. Available from http://www.nrdc.org/nuclear/nudb/datab20.asp.

Norris, Robert S., and Hans M. Kristensen. 2005. India's Nuclear Forces, 2005. *Bulletin of the Atomic Scientists*:73-75.

Norris, Robert S., and Hans M. Kristensen. 2007. India's Nuclear Forces, 2007. *Bulletin of the Atomic Scientists*:74-78.

Nunn, Sam. 2006. Nuclear Pig in a Poke. *Wall Street Journal*, 24 May.

Olweus, Dan. 1991. Bully/Victim Problems Among Schoolchildren: Basic facts and effects of a school based intervention program. In *The Development and Treatment of Childhood Aggression*, edited by D. Peplar and K. Rubin. Hillsdale, NJ: Erlbaum.

OPANAL. 2007. *Treaty of Bangkok 1995* [cited 11 May 2007]. Available from http://www.opanal.org/NWFZ/Bangkok/Bangkok.htm.

Peplar, Debra, Wendy Craig, and Pauli O'Connell. 1999. Understanding Bullying from a Dynamic Systems Perspective. In *The Blackwell Reader in Development Psychology*, edited by A. Slater and D. Muir. London: Blackwell.

Perkovich, George. 2001. *India's Nuclear Bomb: The Impact on Global Proliferation.* Berkeley, CA: University of California Press.

Poloz, Stephen S. 2007. *Will Canada-India trade blossom?* Export Development Canada, 29 March 2006 [cited 20 August 2007]. Available from http://www.edc.ca/english/docs/ereports/commentary/publications_9754.htm.

Prasad, Jayant. 2006a. Statement. Permanent Mission of India to the Conference on Disarmament. Paper read at Conference on Disarmament, 2 March, at Geneva, Switzerland.

Prasad, Jayant. 2006b. Statement. Permanent Mission of India to the Conference on Disarmament. Paper read at Conference on Disarmament, 17 May, at Geneva, Switzerland.

Prasad, Jayant. 2006c. Statement on agenda item: Effective international arrangements to assure Non-Nuclear Weapon States against the use or threat of use of Nuclear Weapons. Paper read at Permanent Mission of India to the Conference on Disarmament, 3 August, at Geneva, Switzerland.

Prasad, Jayant. 2006d. Statement on transparency in armaments. Paper read at Permanent Mission of India to the Conference on Disarmament, 23 August, at Geneva, Switzerland.

Rajaraman, R. 2005a. Cap the Nuclear Arsenal Now. *The Hindu*, January 25.

Rajaraman, R. 2005b. India-U.S. deal and the Nuclear Ceiling. *The Hindu*, September 10.

Rajaraman, R. 2005c. Split the Atomic. *The Hindustan Times*, November 22.

Rajaraman, R. 2007. A fruitless venture. *The Hindustan Times*, May 1.

Rethinaraj, TS Gopi. 2002. Nuclear diplomacy returns to South Asian security agenda. *Jane's Intelligence Review:*40-43.

Shultz, George P., William J. Perry, and Sam Nunn. 2007. A World Free of Nuclear Weapons *Wall Street Journal*, 4 January.

Sikri, Rajiv. 2006. Nuclear deal: The road ahead for India. *Rediff India Abroad*, 21 December.

Singh, Jaswant. 1999. Clarifying India's nascent nuclear doctrine: An interview with Indian foreign Minister Jaswant Singh. *Arms Control Today*.

Singh, Manmohan. 2007. *Address by Dr. Manmohan Singh, Prime Minister of India at Golden Jubilee function of the Department of Atomic Energy, Kalpakkam, India* Prime Minister's Office, 23 October 2004 [cited 2 August 2007]. Available from http://pmindia.nic.in/speech/content.asp?id=36.

Singh, Natwar. 2005. Inaugural Address by Mr. K. Natwar Singh, Minister of External Affairs of India on "India and the NPT" at the conference on Emerging Nuclear Proliferation Challenges organised by the Institute for Defense Studies and Analyses and Pugwash-India. Paper read at Conference on Disarmament, 5 April 2005, at New Delhi, India.

Spector, Leonard S. 2006. Canada needs to get tough with India. *Toronto Star*, 29 December.

Spector, Leonard S., and Aubrie Ohide. 2005. Negative Security Assurances: Revisiting the Nuclear-Weapons-Free Zone Option. *Arms Control Today*.

Squassoni, Sarah, and Jill Marie Parillo. 2006. US-India Nuclear Cooperation: A Side-by-Side Comparison of Current Legislation. Washington DC: Congressional Research Service.

Squassoni, Sharon. 2006. India and Iran: WMD Proliferation Activities. In *CRS Report for Congress*. Washington, DC: Congressional Research Service.

Subramanian, T.S. 2005. Identifying a civilian nuclear facility is India's decision. *The Hindu*, August 12.

Tellis, Ashley. 2001. India's Emerging Nuclear Posture: Between Recessed Deterrent and Ready Arsenal. In *RAND Research Brief*: RAND Corporation.

Tellis, Ashley. 2006. Atoms for War: US-Indian Civilian Nuclear Cooperation and India's Nuclear Arsenal. New York, NY: Carnegie Endowment for International Peace.

Touhey, Ryan. 2006. Dealing with the peacock: India in Canadian foreign relations, 1941-1976, Political Science, University of Waterloo, Waterloo, ON.

United Nations. 2007. *Resolution 1172* 1998 [cited 11 May 2007]. Available from http://www.un.org/Docs/scres/1998/scres98.htm.

United Nations. 2004. Resolution 1540, edited by U. N. S. Council: United Nations.

US Consulate in Chennai. 2007. *Indian Police Officials Graduate U.S.-Sponsored Antiterrorism Program* United States Consulate in Chennai, 24 January 2006 [cited 4 August 2007]. Available from http://chennai.usconsulate.gov/prind060124.html.

US Department of State. 2007. *Agreement Between The United States of America and The International Atomic Energy Agency for the Application of Safeguards in the United States (and Protocol Thereto)* nd [cited 22 June 2007]. Available from http://www.state.gov/t/ac/trt/5209.htm.

US State Department. 2007. *U.S.-India Civilian Nuclear Cooperation, Fact Sheet* 2005a [cited 2 May 2007]. Available from http://www.state.gov/r/pa/prs/ps/2005/49969.htm.

US State Department. 2007. *Administration to seek Congress' support for nuclear pact with India* 2005b [cited 11 June 2007]. Available from http://usinfo.state.gov/sa/Archive/2005/Jul/20-858577.html.

Webster, Paul. 2006. No Can-Do? *Bulletin of the Atomic Scientists* 62 (1):18-19.

White House. 2007. *Joint Statement between President George W. Bush and Prime Minister Manmohan Singh* 18 July 2005 [cited 6 July 2007]. Available from http://www.whitehouse.gov/news/releases/2005/07/print/200 50718-6.html.

White House. 2007. *India Civil Nuclear Cooperation: Responding to Critics* White House, US Government, 8 March 2006 [cited 22 July 2007]. Available from www.whitehouse.gov/news/releases/2006/03/20060308-3.html.